THE ENGLISH COAST

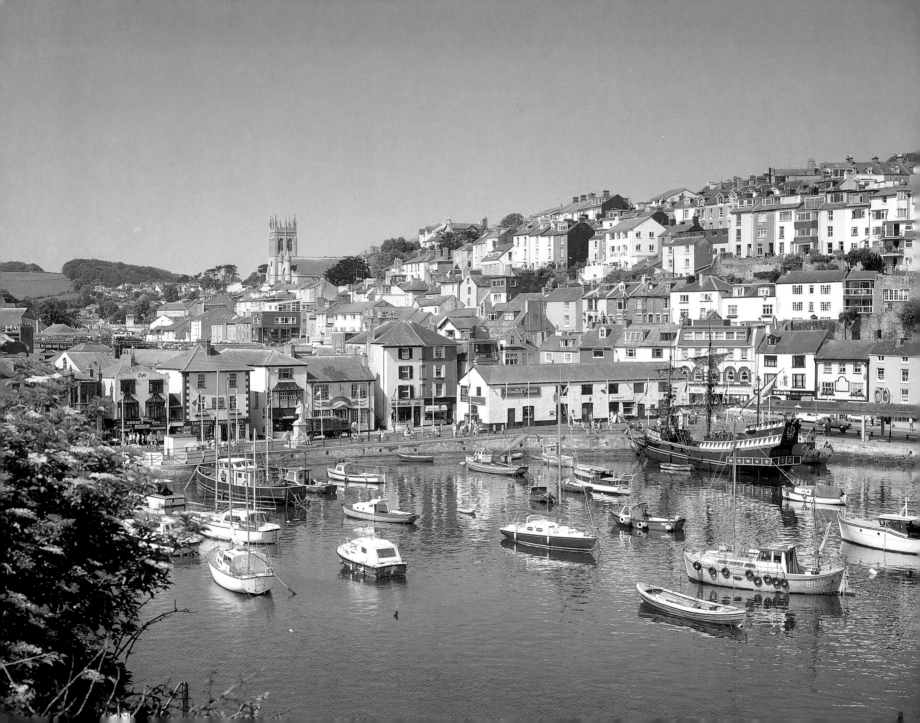

THE ENGLISH COAST

Photographs by JOHN BETHELL
Text by CHRISTOPHER SOMERVILLE

Weidenfeld & Nicolson
London

Photographs © John Bethell 1989
Text © Christopher Somerville 1989

First published in Great Britain by George Weidenfeld and
Nicolson Limited, Orion House, 5 Upper St Martin's Lane,
London WC2H 9EA

First published in hardback as *English Harbours and Coastal Villages*

Half-title page: Buoys in the Trinity House depot at Harwich, Essex
Title page: Brixham, Devon

Printed and bound in Italy

Contents

Author's Acknowledgements

In searching out bits and pieces of local information, these kind people gave us invaluable help: Louise of Cheshire Information Service (Ellesmere Port); Mrs Beck of Maryport and Captain Fortune of Blyth (fishing information); Mr Lyons of Carr's Flour Mill, Silloth; Mr Bailey of Newhaven (the pier light-hut); Heather Howard of Mersea Island (oyster fishing); Arthur Percival and Hugh Perks (copious details about Faversham's Big Building); and Miss Joyce Greenham of Newquay – busy setting up the excellent Gallery of Old Newquay on Chapel Hill, an exhibition to delight visitors and locals alike – who ferreted out as much as is known about that enigmatic Huer's House.

THE ENGLISH COASTLINE

Map showing the location of places illustrated in this book.

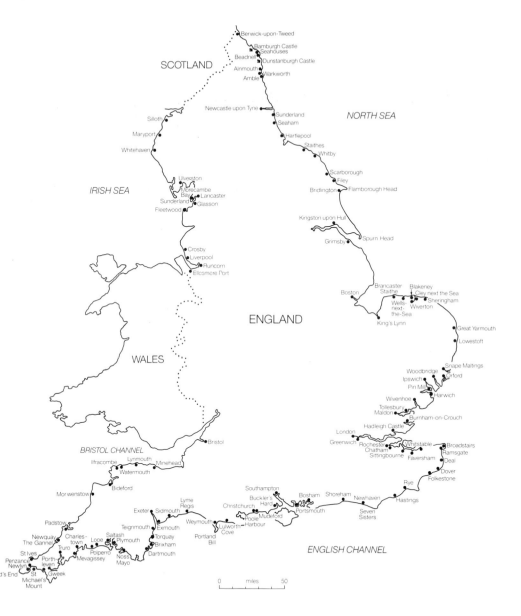

SCOTLAND

Berwick-upon-Tweed
Bamburgh Castle
Seahouses
Beadnell
Dunstanburgh Castle
Alnmouth
Warkworth
Amble

Silloth

Newcastle upon Tyne
Sunderland
Seaham
Maryport

Hartlepool
Whitehaven
Staithes
Whitby

NORTH SEA

Scarborough
Filey
Ulverston
Morecambe
Bay
Lancaster
Bridlington
Flamborough Head

Sunderland
Glasson
Fleetwood

Kingston upon Hull
Spurn Head
Grimsby

IRISH SEA

Crosby
Liverpool
Runcorn
Ellesmere Port

Boston
Brancaster
Staithe
Blakeney
Cley next the Sea
Sheringham
Wells-
next-
the-Sea
Wiverton

ENGLAND

King's Lynn

Great Yarmouth
Lowestoft

WALES

Snape Maltings
Woodbridge
Orford
Ipswich
Pin Mill
Wivenhoe
Harwich
Tollesbury
Maldon
Burnham-on-Crouch
London
Hadleigh Castle
Greenwich
Rochester
Whitstable
Broadstairs
Chatham
Ramsgate
Sittingbourne
Faversham
Deal
Dover
Folkestone
Rye
Hastings
Newhaven
Seven
Sisters

Bristol

BRISTOL CHANNEL

Ilfracombe
Lynmouth
Minehead
Watermouth

Morwenstow
Bideford

Southampton
Buckler's
Hard
Bosham
Shoreham
Christchurch
Portsmouth
Lyme
Regis

Padstow
Exeter
Sidmouth
Weymouth
Mudeford
Poole
Harbour
Lulworth
Cove
Portland
Bill
Newquay
The Gannel
Charles-
town
Looe
Saltash
Teignmouth
Exmouth
Truro
Plymouth
Torquay
St Ives
Polperro
Brixham
Penzance
Porth-
leven
Mevagissey
Noss
Dartmouth
Newlyn
St
Mayo
Land's End
Michael's
Gweek
Mount

ENGLISH CHANNEL

0   miles   50

Introduction

*T*o an island people like the English there's something eternally fascinating about the ports, harbours and villages of their coastline. Down the centuries, from these docks, quaysides and jetties, the island has thrown out lines of communication to the outside world – two-way lines of trade, exploration, fishing and warfare.

Into English docks have come new and exotic items at their appropriate moments in history: the potato, the tomato, and tobacco; strange metals and woods; music, art and literature; heroes and murderers, saints and rogues; people of all degrees of eminence from all nations and corners of the globe. Out have poured wool, textiles, metal goods, fine furniture, salt herrings, tin ingots, coal and cutlery, supplied by England to just about everywhere else.

Buildings that stand on quaysides today in places like Whitby, Boston, Dartmouth and Plymouth witnessed the start of voyages and journeys that would open up and change the world. The great naval bases saw off and welcomed home victorious navies and defeated armies. They built, repaired and sent to sea again the famous ships of the past – *Victory, Agamemnon, Endeavour, Ark Royal, Golden Hind*. Both trading ports and naval bases suffered terrible destruction from raids, fire, sword and bombardment from sea and air. When the English weren't fighting foreigners, they were usually fighting each other and attacking each other's forts and castles. Meanwhile, from ordinary fishing villages went out ordinary people to perform heroic deeds of rescue in fishing boats and lifeboats, and to work weary hours of heavy, lonely and dangerous labour to bring back the silver harvest.

The towns and villages of the English coastline are laden with the drama and power of over two thousand years of history. This book sets out on a journey to discover that history: the great days of sea trade with America, the West Indies, the Baltic countries and the Mediterranean; tales of deep-sea whaling and herring fishing; proud navies setting out to fight famous sea battles; humble ships slipping quietly away to find fresh worlds. To stand, surrounded by the empty marshland of a remote Lancashire coast, on a weather-worn quay where

Britain's very first consignment of raw cotton from the New World was landed, and to reflect on how King Cotton was to change the whole face of northern England, is to savour the very spice of history. You can feel the same excitement when exploring Isambard Kingdom Brunel's revolutionary steamship SS *Great Britain*, returned to Bristol from service, shipwreck and abandonment, and now back in the same dry dock in which she was built a century and a half ago; and on hearing your own footsteps on the cobbles trodden by the Pilgrim Fathers as they walked down the quay at Plymouth towards the waiting *Mayflower*.

Our journey starts in a canal basin on the River Mersey, 10 miles from the coast – not a place most people would think of as a port, perhaps, but then there are quite a few such surprises in this book. From the Mersey we pass the once mighty, then derelict, now reviving (in a very different guise) dockland of Liverpool, the sandy coastline of Lancashire and the Fylde peninsula, where Fleetwood's trawler fleet is based next door to Blackpool, Britain's biggest and brashest seaside resort. Then come tiny, forgotten ports on the windy, muddy inlets of the little-visited Lune estuary below the great flat sweep of Morecambe Bay, and the southern spurs of Lakeland merging with the long curve of red sandstone cliffs that border the western shores of Cumbria. Here the remote coal and ore ports stand in obsolescence and isolation, like full stops on a line that at last reaches the wide Solway Firth and a view across to the blue hills of Galloway.

From the eastern end of the Scottish border the journey sets off again, southwards along Northumberland's long, deserted beaches of sand where the fishing villages stand in crevices of low cliffs. Then an entirely different world approaches: the coal-bearing landscape of the north-east with its coal ports, all now either completely shorn of their trade or in decline as the pits that once served them shut down; and the great shipbuilding rivers of Tyne and Wear, where at Newcastle and Sunderland a sad skeleton of the once-healthy shipyards still just about twitches. Then comes industrial Teesside, followed by the indented run down Yorkshire's mineral-rich cliffs with their marvellously picturesque working fishing villages like Staithes, and big resort towns such as Scarborough and Bridlington. Now appears that long stretch of geometrically regular Humberside coastline where the villages and small resorts are steadily losing their surrounding fields and, from time to time, bits of themselves to the sea, as the eastern coast of England dips a centimetre or so each year in response to the rise of the western coast, and the crumbling cliffs give in to the insistent attacks of the ever-hungry North Sea. The route passes the refineries and fish docks in the mouth of the River Humber (and takes a short detour inland to Hull's busy waterfront), and then enters the mostly unvisited, low-lying, sparsely populated coastline of Lincolnshire.

At the Wash the coast turns north and east for the great bulge of East Anglia, the shingled, sanded and silted ex-harbours (now peaceful yachting havens) of north Norfolk, and the tottering cliffs towards Great Yarmouth. Then the reverse sweep of Suffolk, with Lowestoft and its trawlers, Harwich and its shocking red lightships and buoys, breaks up into the complex of muddy, lonely creeks, salt marshes and sea walls of the Essex coast, where the little old oyster-fishing villages make a new living out of weekending and commuting Londoners. We pay a call at the refurbishing, gentrifying, reviving London dockland, before heading out along the Thames estuary, round the chalk nose of North Foreland and Dickens's Broadstairs, to turn west for the great run along the southern shore of England.

Here are the Channel ports, waiting for the Channel Tunnel to bring them joy or despair, prosperity or wholesale unemployment; the sprawling, sixty-mile strip of built-up coast that ends at Chichester Harbour's wide and peaceful waters; more sprawl, bustle and clamour at the dockyards and quaysides of Portsmouth and Southampton; more wide waters in Poole Harbour; and then the chalk cliffs, heavy with clay, turning to limestone and sandstone as they march west past the cream tea resorts of Weymouth, Lyme Regis and Sidmouth to reach the broad estuary of the River Exe.

The last leg of the journey – a dog-leg – is around the toe of England, the south-west's long peninsula, and takes in Brixham's trawlers and yachts behind its stupendous breakwater; Dartmouth tucked away up its river; the historic western-most seaport, Plymouth; and the classic holiday villages of Cornwall, where work and play have to co-exist and where fishing is still a vital part of the economy – and not just because it looks good on Kodachrome. This round-England trip ends with north Devon's heavenly coast of rounded green and red cliffs and Somerset's coast of cliff and marsh, before making a grand approach up the Severn estuary to come to a halt in Bristol, for centuries England's premier seaport.

It is interesting to note that of England's 'big three ports' – Liverpool, Bristol and London – the last two flourished in situations several miles from the open sea. Ease of communication with the rest of the country was of paramount importance in import and export of goods and passengers. The tedious (and, in Bristol's case, narrow and tortuous) journey upriver from the sea was offset by the efficient and long-established system of roads enjoyed by these two ancient cities and by their already thriving markets. All the same, it took the establishment of a proper docks system in both places to bring the best out of them.

If all England's magnificent diversity of coastline, the enormous variety of ports, harbours and coastal villages, added up to nothing more than a succession of pretty postcards or historical showplaces, then this would be a rather sad and sterile journey. But these places are still vibrantly alive, notwithstanding the great changes that they have all had to face up to. They are still very much at the sharp edge of things, as they always were. Almost everything has changed in the last century, however, replacing confidence with uncertainty and self-belief with anxiety. Wars, recessions, changing tastes, competition from overseas markets have all combined to reduce drastically many of England's traditional imports and exports while some – like tin, and salt herrings – have been brought almost to the point of extinction. The fleets of coastal shipping that used to transport everything from coals to candles around our shores have dwindled away, with road and rail stealing their business. In the great ports, where, against all the bustle of activity and profit-making, the age-old trade of fishing always went on quietly from some obscure jetty or behind a coal staithe, the fishing fleets now – especially those of the North Sea – are barred from their traditional waters, hemmed in by EEC quotas and finding themselves competing with deadly efficiency for not nearly enough fish stocks to go round.

Some changes are bitterly resented by communities which are not powerful enough to resist them. Chief of these is 'yuppification', the patronising 'discovery' and all-too-often insensitive invasion of a place by rich outsiders, so clearly seen in those grand marina plans for fading harbours and in the prevalence of holiday cottages in the north Norfolk and south coast villages, where every other house is a second home and the village centre is devoid of life except on summer weekends. This problem isn't

WELLS-NEXT-THE-SEA, NORFOLK

Rising over the harbour waters and salt marshes of Wells-next-the-Sea, a boiling mass of clouds, stained orange by a typically vivid East Anglian sunset, shows where a North Sea storm is brewing up.

just confined to the coast, but it displays itself especially vividly there, where tradition knits communities so tightly together. Solid, bedrock ways of life with their familiar buildings, customs and other trappings are felt to be slipping away – be they pilchard fishing, granite export or barley malting – and are being replaced by something less personal, less local in flavour and a good deal less substantial. It's the effect of replacing work with play.

The knack of seeing a new trend and grasping its possibilities, however, has always been one of the great strengths of our coastal communities. They have always been eager to exploit the various commerical strands thrown them throughout history, such as the American trade, Baltic trade, whaling, shipbuilding, and the coal-, ore- and cloth-handling trades. Now they are turning, one and all in their individual ways, to the twentieth century's fastest booming industry: tourism. These days the ports and harbours look to tourism to provide the butter on their bread – and, more and more, to provide the bread itself. This is especially true in the beach-girt, cliff-encircled West Country, which has been at it for over a century. But places with far fewer natural assets – the Cumbrian and Durham coal ports, for example, or the Merseyside canal ports – are beginning to look with a fresh eye at fixtures that only a couple of decades ago were considered eyesores: old warehouses, dock offices, cranes, disused vessel basins, towering industrial chimneys, rope stores, derelict fishing boats, net lofts, and even Grandfather's sea boots for the new maritime museum. Almost anything that can conceivably be thought of as an asset, something to attract a visitor's interest, is hunted down and refurbished. Who could have predicted in the 1960s that anyone in their right minds would want to spend a day in Liverpool's Albert Dock, or lay out hundreds of thousands of pounds on a flat in an old spice warehouse in Wapping? Yet it has happened, in response to a reawakening of interest in the craftsmanship, solidity and confidence of the artifacts and lifestyles of past generations, and the contact they give us with our own history – a contact so easy to let slip, as the bulldozers break down Victorian streets and the transatlantic-style megashops cover the acres of green fields at the edge of town.

Ports, harbours and fishing villages are great places to hold up the uncertain present to the steady light of the past. The coastal communities are engaged on what is turning out to be the toughest in two thousand years of tough challenges: to keep worthwhile traditions alive, to exhibit the carcasses of the dead ones as tastefully as possible to interested visitors, and to gear themselves up for a rewarding but unpredictable new way of life while keeping their feet firmly bedded on the reliable old one. How they are getting on you will discover, as you set out from Ellesmere Port to Bristol by way of Flamborough Head.

The North-West Coast

RUNCORN, CHESHIRE

Tug boats lie in wait for great cargo vessels making their way up and down the Manchester Ship Canal. Completed in 1894 to carry Manchester's textiles to an eager world via the sea, the ship canal is still heavily used. Runcorn bridge, in the background, leaps gracefully over the canal and the River Mersey. When opened in 1961, the bridge with its 1,082ft span was the third largest of its kind in the world. But for the local people that extravagant statistic couldn't make good the loss of its much-loved predecessor, a transporter bridge that featured a moving car crossing canal and river on cables.

*F*acing west into the Atlantic Ocean and towards America, while sheltering in the lee of Ireland, the north-west coast has strong links with the New World in the older ports. Liverpool dominates this particular slice of trading history, having grown rich during the eighteenth century on the produce of British possessions – especially the West Indies. The exotic stuff that came pouring in through Liverpool's docks, which included everything from lemons to raw cotton, was balanced by the workaday output of the industrial north – machines and cloth. There was something less workaday, too: slaves, packed hundreds together in airless tiers in the holds of stinking slaveships, which local seamen could smell as they lay out in the Mersey, waiting for a wind.

Liverpool was lucky with its position, situated on both a navigable river and on the sea. But not all ports are coastal. Many miles up the Mersey are river ports – Ellesmere Port and Runcorn – that benefited from the canal traffic which threaded its way along the canals of midland and northern England all through the Industrial Revolution and long afterwards. Further north, Lancaster's transatlantic and coastal trade boomed, too, once the city had run a branch from its Preston canal westwards to the sea. But for decades Lancaster had already been in contact with sea trade, by means of its own quays nearly ten miles up the River Lune, as well as its little subsidiary ports of Sunderland and Glasson, down on the coast in the river's estuary.

The urge to establish a sea connection, to get a grip on desirable New World commodities with one hand and pass over one's own home-grown produce with the other, is a constant theme among the ports of the north-west coast. Trading coal to a coal-less Ireland also became enormous business for those ports up on the Cumbrian coast, like Whitehaven and Maryport, built by owners of nearby coalmines. Ores from the Cumbrian hills were also gobbled up greedily by the industrial cities of England, bringing more business to these ports.

Fishing went on side by side with all the trading and industrial activity. Fishermen in Morecambe Bay had all they needed on their doorsteps, under the sands or in the great waters of the bay, while from the 1830s onwards the fishermen of Fleetwood went further and further out – to Iceland late in the century, when Grimsby trawler firms came round the coast to show them how.

So much for the busy past. The Merseyside canal and river ports are still industrial and commercial centres, though a lot of their business comes by road these days. Fleetwood trawlers catch a lot of fish, though less than they did before the Cod War with Iceland and subsequent contraction of available fishing grounds. Irish boats base themselves alongside Whitehaven's fleet in that town's harbour. But the last liners have left the Mersey long since, and the Liverpool docks stand mostly idle. The Ulverston canal, the quays at Glasson, the harbour basin at Maryport – these handle no more cargoes, while the quays by the Lune at Lancaster are for strollers and youthful anglers.

Leisure, on the other hand, becomes bigger and bigger business. Here, on a coast which most tourists know only for Blackpool and Morecambe, towns with their traditional industries dying or dead have to work tremendously hard to achieve the metamorphosis into places that people want to visit. Merseyside Development Corporation have caught on to the potential in their miles of derelict dockland; the renovation of the Albert Dock is a model of its kind. The harbour basins at Maryport and Glasson are full of yachts and sailing dinghies. One of the most run-down and doldrum-hit ports, Maryport, has a maritime museum to attract the tourists. Whitehaven is smartening up its decayed Georgian streets with the help of money from industry.

This north-western end of the country does not, however, attract the kind of City money and hard-nosed opportunism that generates those 'exclusive waterside village complete with own marina' schemes for depressed resorts in the golden south-east. Maybe it's just as well. You can still walk out in the middle of Morecambe Sands and feel as lonely as on any felltop in nearby Lakeland. And a crumbling, silt-choked, marshy, silent old port like the Lancashire Sunderland, lying half-vanished among tidal creeks and acres of spartina grass, bears witness to a process – in many ways more encouraging than disheartening in this overcrowded, over-built age – that puts all insubstantial endeavour into proper perspective: nature's gentle, unstoppable recapture of ground that man has appropriated, altered, used, and finally abandoned.

ELLESMERE PORT, CHESHIRE

The world's largest collection of narrowboats is kept at the National Waterways Museum, Ellesmere Port. Here the Shropshire Union Canal meets the Manchester Ship Canal on the south bank of the River Mersey. The Shropshire Union's drive to break through to the Mersey at the turn of the nineteenth century brought Ellesmere Port into being as a complex of locks, docks and wharves. Railways came, too, and in their turn, oil refineries, power stations, storage tanks, pylons, cement works and sewage works – all still there beside the Mersey, but all out of sight and out of mind in the calm, watery acres of the Waterways Museum.

LIVERPOOL, MERSEYSIDE

The Birkenhead ferry plies across the broad River Mersey towards George's Landing Stage at Liverpool's famous Pierhead. The buildings that stand here – the Royal Liver Building of 1910 with its 295ft twin towers topped with the splendid Liver Birds, the Cunard Building of 1916 and the 1907 Dock Board Offices, together with the Town Hall's green dome rising behind – were landmarks and symbols of defiance to sailors returning from Atlantic convoys in 1940–41, when bombing raids were changing every other aspect of this great seaport.

ALBERT DOCK, LIVERPOOL, MERSEYSIDE

A warm brick hymn to the Victorians' confidence in trade, Liverpool's Albert Dock was opened in 1846 by the Prince Consort himself. Half a century later, as Albert's widow was coming to the end of her long reign, the 68-acre complex was already obsolete, its basins and entrances too small to cope with the huge new iron steamships. By 1981 nearly a thousand acres of Liverpool dockland lay derelict. Merseyside Development Corporation, formed in that year to encourage the moribund dockland to its feet, is massaging life back into the waterfront, though of a sort the old dockers would hardly recognize. Four hundred thousand tons of mud were dredged out of the Albert Dock; winebars, restaurants, a maritime museum, upmarket shops, offices and even an outstation of the Tate Gallery have all been opened in the refurbished warehouses.

FLEETWOOD, LANCASHIRE

The nets and floats of the fishing fleet lie in a jumble on the quayside at Fleetwood, one of the biggest fishing ports in England. From here large deep-sea trawlers go far out in search of the cod and haddock that still abound in some of the roughest and coldest waters in the world off Iceland and Greenland. Fleetwood's fish dock covers many acres, and the town's economy is still founded on fishing. But since 1975, when Iceland extended its fishing limits, Fleetwood's trawlers have been feeling the pinch.

To help protect the Fleetwood trawlermen against the chills of far northern seas, an enterprising company developed the 'Fisherman's Friend', a throat lozenge strong enough to stun a whale. Britain's schoolchildren hold the name of Fleetwood, featured on the packet, in awe. There is a popular playground challenge: eat three Fisherman's Friends in a row without crying.

FLEETWOOD, LANCASHIRE

A trawler enters the estuary of the River Wyre after a night's fishing in the Irish Sea, thankful to be passing the familiar blue outlines of the Pennine hills.

Fleetwood town was built brand new in the 1830s by the local landowner Sir Peter Hesketh-Fleetwood. Its great tradition of deep-sea trawling was established half a century later, when a long-sighted Grimsby trawling concern opened up a branch at Fleetwood, which was nearer than the east coast to the teeming Icelandic fishing grounds. Since then sail, steam and diesel have taken successive generations of Fleetwood trawlermen to the far north in search of the silver harvest.

GLASSON, LANCASHIRE

This cut joins the Preston-to-Lancaster Canal with Glasson dock, seen in the distance. Glasson lies in a sheltered crook of the River Lune where it bends south to enter the Irish Sea. Glasson was perfectly placed to become the coastal port of the city of Lancaster late in the eighteenth century, when woollen and cotton goods from Lancashire's textile mills, and fine furniture from its workshops, were pouring out for export. At the same time, Britain's possessions in the West Indies were sending back a steady flood of sugar, rum, fruit, raw cotton (for the mills) and hardwoods (for the workshops).

The view in this photograph, seen then, would have been a mass of merchantmen's crossed yards and rigging. These days the sandstone quays and the warehouses, pubs and cottages of the purpose-built river port see only the slender masts of pleasure yachts.

ST GEORGE'S QUAY, LANCASTER, LANCASHIRE

A favourite stroll for the citizens of Lancaster is along St George's Quay, under the trees and past the old warehouses built in the eighteenth century days of West Indian trade, when more goods passed through the port of Lancaster than the port of Liverpool. The River Lune, tidal as far inland as Lancaster, gave up the fight in the end against silt and the emergence of Liverpool's docks, but it still yields many a flounder and eel, and even the occasional salmon, to the lures of young local anglers on the quay.

SUNDERLAND, LANCASHIRE

Above a muddy foreshore, a single line of houses stands as a reminder of the days in the early eighteenth century when this lonely spot on the Lune estuary was the port of Sunderland, through which Lancaster traded with the West Indies. The very first bale of raw cotton to be fed into the soon insatiable maw of the textile mills of Lancashire was landed here. Robert Lawson, a Quaker merchant, built the port with, among other materials, sandstone blocks from the ruins of Cockersand Abbey just across the estuary – waste not, want not. Some of the original warehouses still stand, proof of the excellence of monkish masonry.

MORECAMBE BAY, LANCASHIRE

Sandstone strata emerge from the low shoreline cliffs at Heysham, Lancashire, from where more than a hundred square miles of dead flat sands spread out around the enormous disc of Morecambe Bay. Hundreds of thousands of sea birds and waders come to feed on the marine organisms that live beneath the sands. Adventurous walkers can make an exciting crossing of the Bay under the watchful eye of the Sands Guide. This is a magnificent place of vast views and skyscapes (the southern fells of Lakeland are seen on the distant horizon in this photograph), where wind and the piping of waders are the loudest noises. Standing out in the middle of Morecambe Bay, with the sea many miles away across the sands, you can experience what past generations took for granted and we so rarely find – perfect peace.

ULVERSTON, CUMBRIA

When this entrance gate to Ulverston's mile-long canal was opened for traffic in 1796, iron ore mining was bringing high hopes of prosperity to the little south Lakeland market town. The River Leven had long since shrunk away, choked with sand, to leave Ulverston stranded well inland, but the canal would open up a route for sea trade once more. So it proved. Business boomed into the 1840s, with 35,000 tons a year passing along the canal. In 1845 came more business – materials for the building of the Furness Railway, which within twenty years had bought up the canal and sucked away its lifeblood of trade. The corpse of the canal twitched on till a final abandonment at the end of the Second World War – done to death by the rival it had helped to bring into being.

WHITEHAVEN, CUMBRIA

Cradled in the Cumbrian coast's red sandstone cliffs, Whitehaven's harbour basks in late sunlight as cloud thickens over the Galloway hills on the northern skyline. This mass of stone piers and quays was built during the seventeenth and eighteenth centuries by the Lowther family. Whitehaven became Britain's chief coal port, but the industries that made the town prosperous – coal, sandstone, shipbuilding, ironstone – were all overtaken and made obsolete by twentieth century technology. For decades the beautiful, planned Georgian town and its harbour lay desolate and derelict, but new money and new energy have seen Whitehaven pull itself up by its own bootstraps: neglected buildings have been cleaned up, and the harbour welcomes pleasure boats. The new benefactors? Two very modern industries themselves in need of a cleaner image – a chemicals firm and the nearby Sellafield nuclear reprocessing plant.

MARYPORT, CUMBRIA

Another of the planned towns laid out along the Cumbrian coast by local coal-owners in the eighteenth century, Maryport was named after the wife of its founder, Colonel Humphrey Senhouse. The town went into a long slump when its coal seams began to give out. By the 1960s the pits were closed, and so was the harbour. Unlike Whitehaven, Maryport has had no fairy industrial godmothers to smarten her up. The town has made an effort with tourism – a maritime museum in Senhouse Street, good beaches nearby, and a yacht haven in the old local basin. The fishing ticks on, too, for cod, sole, plaice, haddock and skate, and a few lobsters. Fishermen's co-operatives have been started, abandoned and started again. Out on this remote coast, far from any major town, Maryport is a prime example of the struggle to survive faced by such settlements, built for a purpose that history has cancelled.

SILLOTH, CUMBRIA

Uncompromising utility is the keynote of this fine shot of Carr's Flour Mill at Silloth, sited on an isolated stretch of the Solway Firth where England stares across at Scotland. 'Silloth-on-Solway' was the port for Carlisle in the 1850s, but soon settled back into a respectable role as a small resort.

The red brick Carr's mill, built in 1886 with its own sidings and dock, still takes grain from ships unloading at its wharf – as seen here – and sends its flour all over the country. Some goes east to Carlisle, where it is baked in Carr's biscuit factory to make some of the finest water biscuits ever to meet cheese.

The North Sea Coast

STAITHES, YORKSHIRE

Artists love Staithes, and no wonder. Visitors love it too – and no wonder, either. Its maze of steep, cobbled streets, piled-up cottages with red pantiled roofs, snug old pubs, fishing harbour and winding beck between spectacular headlands were made for canvas and camera. The Captain Cook connection is irresistible as well. As a teenager, apprenticed to a Staithes grocer, young James Cook was so starstruck by local fishermen's yarns of a life on the ocean wave that he ran away to Whitby and signed on as a cabin boy.

Staithes harbour is very much a working place, in spite of its picturesqueness, and those cobles with pointed ends have to cope with menacing winter storms. In the days before tourism Staithes had other strings to its bow beside fishing, for the cliffs around are rich in alum, potash, iron ore and jet. When the markets for these declined earlier this century, tourism arrived.

*F*rom Berwick-upon-Tweed on the Scottish border down to Boston on the Wash is well over 200 miles of coastline, encompassing the empty beaches and coal ports of Northumberland, the fishing harbours and seaside resorts of Yorkshire, the chalk headlands and industrial sprawl of Humberside, and the long, crumbling Lincolnshire coast. What knits all this diversity of landscape and activity together is the encroaching North Sea, so keen to eat into this east-facing shore. A lot of clay, a lot of chalk and a lot of sand are mixed up in the eastern edges of England – stuff that the North Sea's ferocious winter gales and pounding seas consume at a rate of several yards a year in Humberside and Lincolnshire.

Past industries, whose remnants are found on the North Sea coast, tended to be rather more parochial than the great transatlantic bargainings of the north-west coast's ports. Coal strikes the key note – coal that flowed like a never-ceasing, solid black river out of the Northumberland and Durham coalfields, down the wooden waggonways of the seventeenth and eighteenth centuries and the iron railways of the nineteenth and twentieth, to the big loading platforms known as 'staithes' at Amble, Sunderland, Seaham, Hartlepool and, above all, Newcastle upon Tyne, and thence out in the grubby coal boats to power the Industrial Revolution. The collier boats were a familiar sight all round Britain's shores, until railway and road took their trade. New technology eventually made coal look old-fashioned, dirty and inefficient anyway. A certain amount of coal was exported, unlike the lime produced in Beadnell's great kilns, which was destined for the acid soils of the home market. Popular with customers on the far side of the North Sea were the salt herrings from Seahouses, Hartlepool and Grimsby.

The fishing industry, on the whole, is still a significant part of the life of North Sea coast ports and harbours, though a sad shadow of its former self in the opinion of those old enough to remember the pre-war boom days of steam drifters and herring glut. Bridlington, Hull and Grimsby send out their trawlers to the deep-sea grounds, Seahouses its smaller boats after whitefish closer to shore; pots are set, and crabs and lobsters taken by cobles, from Beadnell down to Flamborough. At Berwick-upon-Tweed and Amble the salmon fall to the nets of estuary fishermen. The sophistication of the fish-finding gear on board the larger trawlers, in fact, brings success on too grand a scale, for the fish stocks of the North Sea are disappearing at an alarming rate into their big nets. The gross pollution of the North Sea by several 'Dirty Men of Europe' – Britain is generally reckoned the dirtiest of the lot – is starting to take its toll of marine life, too. North Sea coast fishing towns are beginning to feel the pinch, but there's plenty of life in the old trade yet.

The coal ports, however – black, filthy, dusty and always working – have suffered as their pits have closed. An abandoned coal staithe doesn't have quite the aesthetic appeal of an abandoned Georgian warehouse. Attracting tourist attention has never been the purpose of places like Seaham, and it's not easy now. A town with a conveniently split personality like Hartlepool (lovely 'old town', busy industrial West Hartlepool) probably has the best of it in this regard. Hull's docks, too, combine impressive looks with continuing business.

One of only a handful of inland ports on the North Sea coast, Hull owes its importance to its position on the River Humber, which gives access to the Trent, the Ouse and, via the Aire and Calder Canal, England's inland waterways system. Most rivers on this coast don't wind broadly down to the sea in a handily navigable way, but either trickle off (or through) the unstable cliffs or thread their way to the beach between hard rocks. Business in many places is conducted face to face with a sea violent enough at times to snatch whole houses from Yorkshire cliff villages such as Staithes and Robin Hood's Bay, gnaw away the ground under farms on the low clay cliffs of Humberside and north Lincolnshire, and flood the low-lying fenland of south Lincolnshire for many miles inland. A huge amount of excess material – stones, shingle, sand, chalk, clay, mud – has been washing up and down the east coast for centuries, slowly settling in harbour mouths and river estuaries. Towns like Alnmouth and Boston lost their river traffic to the silting; on the other hand, the shingle spit of Spurn Head in the mouth of the River Humber owes its existence to just this depositing of material.

The North Sea coast is lucky to have so many actual or potential tourist attractions; and here, as everywhere else around the English coastline, those towns with

BAMBURGH CASTLE, NORTHUMBERLAND

Bamburgh Castle is one of the most dramatically sited castles on the English coastline. It perches 150ft up on an outcropping crag of the Whin Sill, looking out to the flat slabs of the Farne Islands a couple of miles offshore. The castle's turbulent history includes several sieges, destruction by gunfire (the first castle ever to be thus humiliated), and a subsequent chequered career as a private house, a paupers' hospital, a training school for servant girls and a home for shipwrecked sailors.

On Inner Farne island, seen distantly on the left, lived and died St Cuthbert of Lindisfarne in the seventh century AD. Grace Darling, daughter of the lighthouse keeper on Longstone (the outermost of the Farnes), became a national heroine overnight when, on 7 September 1838, she rowed out with her father to rescue nine members of the crew of the wrecked steamer *Forfarshire*. Today the Farne Islands are given over to an enormous population of sea birds and to the east coast's only breeding colony of grey seals.

SCARBOROUGH, YORKSHIRE

'A very pretty Sea-port town built on the side of a high hill' was how Celia Fiennes saw Scarborough in 1697. The description still serves very well. South Bay sweeps round to the wall-enclosed harbour, above which the steep old fishing town climbs the flank of the nose-like headland to the dominating twelfth-century castle. Hidden from sight in this photograph is the corresponding curve of North Bay, lined with imposing Victorian hotels near the edge of the cliffs.

Scarborough is a massively popular resort, and deservedly so. Here are traditional seaside amusements, excellent theatres and museums, lively clubs and pubs, superb Regency architecture, parks and woodlands – something for everyone. Only the elderly fishermen grumble, 'EEC quotas . . . young lads these days . . . now, when *I* was that age . . . and so on, as they turn reluctantly (though in most cases with a sigh of relief) from the fishing to the tourist coble trips round the bay.

redundant or changing industries that have something else they can use to advantage haven't been slow to exploit that potential. Examples are: Alnmouth's conversion of old disused granaries to houses, Beadnell's much photographed lime-kilns, Whitby's abbey and Captain Cook connections, the proximity of Seahouses to the Farne Islands, and just about everything at Staithes; sailing at Whitby, Bridlington and Beadnell Bay; caravans on the Lincolnshire cliffs (sidling inland as the crumbling coastline chases them); lighthouse visits on Flamborough Head; and bird-watching in the Humber estuary. The list goes on, and doesn't include the classic tourist attractions such as the castles at Bamburgh, Dunstanburgh and Warkworth, or great resorts like Scarborough and Skegness.

Adaptable, many-faceted places like these face the future with confidence. Things are not so buoyant, however, in Seaham, now shorn of its bottles, its brass and almost all its coal; nor at Sunderland, whose people are as proud and as hard-working (when they get the chance) as ever, but whose last two shipyards are due to close down. The motto of today's North Sea coastal communities seems to be: adapt and thrive – otherwise you won't survive.

BERWICK-UPON-TWEED, NORTHUMBERLAND

A thousand years of independent self-reliance are summed up in this view of Berwick-upon-Tweed, taken from Tweedmouth on the south bank of the River Tweed. Berwick changed hands thirteen times between England and Scotland from 1147 until 1482, when it was finally won – and held – by the English. The town walls seen here were built in the 1760s, but Elizabethan ones still surround most of Berwick. Above the town's red roofs rises the 150ft steeple of the Georgian Town Hall – the top floor of the bell tower was once used to house felons.

The Tweed, still fished for salmon by Berwick men, is spanned by three superb bridges within half a mile of each other: the fifteen-arch sandstone road bridge of 1634, the concrete one of 1928 just upstream, and Robert Stephenson's famous twenty-eight-arch Royal Border railway bridge of 1850.

SEAHOUSES, NORTHUMBERLAND

Seahouses harbour is the biggest on the north Northumberland coast. It was built at the end of the eighteenth century, and enlarged a hundred years later to take advantage of the arrival in east coast waters of the herring shoals that brought prosperity all along these shores. At the turn of this century Seahouses was a busy place, where girls stood in lines beside the barrels along the quay, gutting and packing the catch as it came in. Most of the herring fishing has disappeared today, but Seahouses has put on a new and gaudier hat as a popular resort for Tynesiders. Boats go out on fishing trips, full of anglers and crates of booze, and are also often hired for the short trip to the Farne Islands.

BEADNELL, NORTHUMBERLAND

These great kilns, built of magnesium limestone, dominate the tiny harbour at Beadnell, a few miles south of Seahouses. The kilns were put up at the turn of the nineteenth century to burn limestone quarried in the village, the lime produced being shipped out to less alkaline farmland soils elsewhere. Nowadays the National Trust owns Beadnell's kilns.

There are still one or two crab and lobster fishermen working out of Beadnell harbour, but most of today's villagers are incomers. Beadnell, small and attractive on a wonderful coastline, has had to fight hard not to become a soulless enclave of weekend cottages, all but deserted from autumn until spring. Villagers say they are winning this battle, slowly.

DUNSTANBURGH CASTLE, NORTHUMBERLAND

The Lilburn lookout tower of Dunstanburgh Castle stands starkly on the castle mound above cliffs of black basalt – another strikingly impressive situation for another Northumbrian coastal castle. Dunstanburgh, built early in the fourteenth century, was a ruin two hundred years later after a stormy saga of artillery battles, sieges and imprisonments. Queen Margaret of Anjou, wife of King Henry VI, escaped by rope and boat from a cell in Dunstanburgh. A legend tells of Sir Guy the Seeker, condemned by a mistaken choice to lose his true love and wander round the walls of Dunstanburgh till death released him from the spell. These ruins, jagged and haunting, are the very stuff of romantic history.

ALNMOUTH, NORTHUMBERLAND

Alnmouth lies low among its sandhills, a favourite sailors' haven. The mouth of the River Aln is usually busy with sailing boats skimming round its wide bends. The latter are a comparatively modern creation, after a tremendous storm on Christmas Day 1806 battered a hole in the bank of the river and formed a new mouth. The harbour, once busy with granaries and shipbuilding (not to mention smuggling) was left stranded and silting. Such excitement is untypical of Alnmouth, a resort favoured by Newcastle upon Tyne folk for its peace and quiet. Even John Paul Jones, the American freelance raider, failed to make much of a stir when he bombarded the town in 1779. He took one shot with a cannon at the church spire – and missed.

WARKWORTH AND AMBLE, NORTHUMBERLAND

Warkworth harbour lies at the southern end of the great four-mile arc of sands that sweep down from Alnmouth. Amble-by-the-Sea stands beside the harbour, an old coal port whose wooden staithes, or loading jetties, make excellent angling platforms these days. Coal does still come into Amble: sea coal, washed ashore when offshore seams are disturbed during winter gales. Two miles up the River Coquet, the silhouette of Warkworth Castle can just be made out. The castle was built about the middle of the twelfth century, in a superb defensive position on a tight loop of the Coquet. Sir Henry Percy, the model for Shakespeare's Harry Hotspur, who was killed at the Battle of Shrewsbury in 1403, was born in Warkworth Castle.

NEWCASTLE UPON TYNE, TYNE AND WEAR

Seen from the roadway of Robert Stephenson's High Level Bridge, the Tyne Bridge of 1928 crosses the River Tyne in the centre of Newcastle supported by its characteristic arch, a shape instantly recognised for miles around (the span measures 531ft, and its top is 193ft above the river at high water). You can see it on the labels of bottles of the famed and feared Newcastle Brown Ale, and it was the model for the rather larger Sydney Harbour Bridge. Together with High Level Bridge, Tyne Bridge makes an impressive exhibition of engineering skill in the heart of a city that prided itself for centuries on its shipbuilding, heavy engineering, steel working, coal shipping and other heavy industries. All are gone now, or going, as Newcastle smartens itself up and turns hopefully to the shoppers and tourists.

SUNDERLAND, TYNE AND WEAR

Like other coal ports in the area, Sunderland once had a forest of coal staithes lining the banks of the River Wear. But Sunderland also had its glassmaking, its marine engineering and, above all, its shipbuilding. Sunderland, along with Newcastle upon Tyne, enjoyed just about the highest reputation in the country for building ships fast and well. The cranes rarely stopped still; neither did the shipyard clangour along Wearside.

The river is quieter now. North-East Shipbuilders had only two yards left in Sunderland when the closure order came just before Christmas 1988. Nissan have recently moved into the town, along with other, lighter industries, and there's a new town centre, too. Sunderland's greatest tradition, though, will soon have disappeared – the end of six hundred years of shipbuilding on the Wear.

SEAHAM, COUNTY DURHAM

Fishing cobles lie peacefully in Seaham harbour, which was once a bustling scene of industrial activity with bottleworks, brass foundries and wagon after wagon coming down to the coal ships from the pits. Dawdon Colliery, seen in the background, just about ticks over, but these days, with the last seams of the Durham coalfield being chased far out under the sea, a Seaham lad is as likely to find work fishing as mining.

HARTLEPOOL, COUNTY DURHAM

Clear evening light shines over Hartlepool's old town and sheltered harbour on their curved crab's claw of a peninsula. Above the mellow Georgian houses rises the tower of St Hilda's church, founded in 1188 on the site of a Saxon convent. This peaceful scene is rather different from what lies out of camera across Hartlepool Bay, where the big docks at West Hartlepool receive North Sea oil and gas, iron ore and timber.

Hartlepudlians have always tended to do things their own way. The fishermen, for example, denied the right in olden times to live within the town walls, turned their backs on the old town and built their own community on the Town Moor, calling it Far Field. And, most celebrated of local legends, there was the time that loyal townsmen in Napoleonic days, finding a monkey cast ashore as sole survivor from the wreck of a French ship, promptly hanged it to prove their patriotic zeal.

WHITBY, YORKSHIRE

Like Staithes, Whitby enjoys a Captain Cook connection. Here he lived for nine years in Grape lane, and here he learned his trade as a sailor. From Whitby in 1768 he sailed for Tahiti by way of Cape Horn. His two South Seas expedition ships, *Resolution* and *Endeavour*, were built at Whitby. In Victorian times large numbers of Whitby men went far away to the whaling, but these days their fishing is closer to home. This photograph looks north across Whitby's harbour, behind which the red pantiled roofs of the old town rise to St Mary's parish church, a fine Norman building often overlooked by visitors intent on the far more celebrated clifftop abbey ruins nearby. The church is reached by a lung-racking climb up the 199 steps of Church Stairs, better known locally as Jacob's Ladder.

FILEY, YORKSHIRE

A great curve of chalky clay cliffs forms the backdrop to Filey Bay at the south-eastern corner of Yorkshire. At the feet of these cliffs run six miles of beautiful, firm sand, sheltered from north-east gales by the long, snout-like promontory of Filey Brigg. This was the perfect spot to start a genteel seaside resort in the 1830s. A decade later, Filey's future was assured when the railway arrived. These days, holiday camps have sprouted along the shore south of the town, but Filey remains a snug little resort. Cobles still fish Filey Bay, but in slowly decreasing numbers. Like all their fellows along this coast, the Filey fishermen pack their cobles in summer with as many tourists as they can entice aboard.

FLAMBOROUGH HEAD, HUMBERSIDE

Evening sun touches the sheer chalk cliffs of Flamborough Head on the extreme eastern tip of north Humberside, encircled by a flat calm sea. Conditions are not always like this off the Head, where the North Sea winds and waves can put on some of their ugliest turns. Hence the lighthouse, built in 1806 to warn off ships from the treacherous currents hereabouts. Storm waves have burrowed arches and caves deep into these cliffs. In spite of the constant sea wind, sea birds roost in hundreds of thousands on the hard chalk crevices of the north-facing cliffs – guillemots, puffins, razorbills, fulmars and the raucous, always-shrieking kittiwakes.

BRIDLINGTON, HUMBERSIDE

Bridlington – but no-one calls it anything but 'Brid' – is very much a fishing town and local people's resort. When the railway arrived from Hull in 1846, Brid became a popular place for Yorkshire families to spend a week or two on the sands. It's still just that; few outsiders come to Brid. Brid has become something of a yachting centre in recent years, but the town's trawlermen are proud of their continuing deep-sea calling. Keel boats go pot-fishing out of the harbour, too, and there's always good business in spinning tourists round the bay. Bridlington Bay's shifting tides and winds make it a hazardous place, even for local fishermen. The Bridlington lifeboat crew, like their Flamborough counterpart at North Landing, do their dangerous, essential work with complete modesty and lack of fuss.

SPURN HEAD, HUMBERSIDE

Spurn Head lighthouse, built at the end of the nineteenth century, stands in one of the loneliest spots in Britain – at the end of Spurn's curved spit of sand and pebbles. Three miles long and only a hundred yards wide, the spit bends like an ant-eater's snout across the mouth of the River Humber. For ninety years the lighthouse warned passing sailors off this extremely dangerous obstacle and the ever-moving banks and bars of sand that surround it. In 1985 the light was finally shut off, put into retirement by modern electronic warning devices, much to the disapproval of the Spurn Point coastguard, now 'rationalized' away to Bridlington. The striped tower remains on Spurn Head as a sailors' landmark.

KINGSTON UPON HULL, HUMBERSIDE

Kingston upon Hull's warehouses and wharves along the River Hull present a telling view of a great inland port whose life is entirely bound up with its sea connections. Hull's docks – now occupying a seven-mile stretch of the River Humber – began operating in 1778; and the town, although nearly twenty miles from the coast, was boosted into a position as one of Britain's leading ports. Hull whalers no longer go down to the South Atlantic. Hull trawlers, shut out recently from Icelandic waters, are diminishing in number. But the docks go on from strength to strength, as do the wharves along the River Hull, where the town originally developed. Container cargoes, oil tankers, North Sea ferries, timber and grain vessels, cargo ships of all kinds keep Hull's flavour a strongly salty one.

GRIMSBY, HUMBERSIDE

More than any other of England's famous fishing towns, Grimsby is symbolised by its trawlers. Like Eccles and cakes, or Derby and rams, Grimsby and trawlers go together. The biggest town on the south Humberside coast, and still England's most important seine-netting harbour, Grimsby lands over 200,000 tons of fish a year. There are other landings at Grimsby, too – Danish butter and bacon, for example – but it's fish that keeps the town afloat. The fish market bustles, the gulls gather in thousands over the Fish Dock, the refrigerated lorries roar in and out of town, and Grimsby's streets see more Scandinavians and Icelanders than anywhere else south of the Scottish border.

The Dock Tower of 1852, seen in the background, is a copy of Siena's town hall. It contains an ingenious system for working the dock gates hydraulically, based on an internal water tank.

BOSTON, LINCOLNSHIRE

The muddy River Witham curves through Boston towards the most famous church tower in Lincolnshire: the 272½ ft 'Stump' of St Botolph's Church, which has stood over the Fens since 1460 as a landmark for travellers and a beacon for sailors. When the Stump was built, Boston was a great wool port, but the silting up of the Witham brought centuries of slump and depression to the Fenland town. Dissenters left the old Boston to establish the new one across the Atlantic, giving birth to trade with England's west coast ports that left Boston even deeper in the dumps. But Victorian energy and enterprise came to the rescue, building new docks and a new cut to the sea. Boston Stump is still the town's greatest tourist attraction, though, not least for the view from its summit, gained after a climb of 365 steps, across thirty miles of flat Lincolnshire land to the far-off towers of Lincoln Cathedral.

East Anglia and the Thames Estuary

The bane of England's east coast ports is well seen in the harbour of Wells-next-the-Sea. So many ports here have seen their rivers, harbours and shoreline slip further and further away as sand and shingle block up, strangle and kill off the river mouths and estuaries. The sea approach to Wells is via a right-angle channel, with enormous salt marshes all round, that runs south to the great granary, handsome old pubs and waterfront of what was once a bustling port. A few coasting freighters carrying grain and animal feeds still manage to make their way up to Wells on the highest of spring tides. Now the town chiefly bustles with yachtsmen and tourists – still a centre of activity, but no longer next-the-Sea.

From the Wash down to the Thames estuary, two products have really galvanized the ports and harbours, bringing prosperity during times past: wool, and then fish. The rolling pasturelands of East Anglia were ideal for sheep rearing, and for weaving wool into cloth. Weavers from the Low Countries came across to settle during the Middle Ages – many because of religious persecution at home – and by passing on their skills brought riches to East Anglia that were greater than those enjoyed by any other part of the country. Their influence is still seen in the architecture of former wool ports like King's Lynn, Great Yarmouth and Ipswich, where parts of the waterfronts can seem more Dutch than English.

After the trade in wool and woollen cloth slackened, fishing grew in importance. Great fishing harbours sent out their boats in enormous fleets, King's Lynn men to the whaling (there were blubber sheds in Lynn), Great Yarmouth and Lowestoft men after the 'siller herring'. The kipper girls came down from Scotland every year, following the herring to the gutting sheds and smokeries of the East Anglian fishing towns. These were the famous whitefish ports, but there were thriving shellfish towns and villages all down the muddy creeks and marshlands of Essex and the Thames estuary. Mersea Island, Wivenhoe, Tollesbury, Maldon, Burnham-on-Crouch, Faversham and Whitstable were all places where it was easier to buy oysters than herrings. It was easier to buy good, cheap gin or brandy, too, for smuggling was even bigger business than oysters in this watery, deceptive landscape where only insiders knew all the nooks and crannies.

Other trade, the import and export of all kinds of commodities, swelled business at the big East Anglian docks of Lynn, Yarmouth, Lowestoft and Ipswich, and the Thames-side ones of Rochester and Whitstable. But up until this century almost every coastal town and village had its own little dock or quay, handling a few sacks of grain, a barrel or two of fish, some timber, bricks and sand. Silt put paid to most of them. The whole of the north Norfolk coast bulge is lined with one village after another whose quays stand a mile or more inland, their lifeline rivers now flowing in different channels or clogged almost to a standstill, and their sea borders blocked by acres of marshland composed of deposited silt, knitted together by spartina grass or long-rooted sea purslane. All this silt, shingle and sand that settles in banks and bars drifts westward along the coast from the crumbling, tottering, always yielding cliffs of sand, chalk and clay that run east from Cromer for a dozen miles and more. Large, influential places like Great Yarmouth and Lowestoft received the investment that built piers, jetties and other silt-repelling devices, but little country villages could only stand by and watch their sea link lengthen, weaken and finally snap.

These villages today, left in enforced retirement, stay healthy on a mixed diet of tourists, commuters and weekenders; though some of them are finding these last more indigestible then they had bargained for. In winter hardly a light shines along the main street of some north Norfolk villages. From Brancaster Staithe to Burnham-on-Crouch any basin or strip of river left unclogged by silt is crammed with yachts and sailing dinghies. Visitors come for the sailing, for the wildlife sanctuaries of Blakeney Spit, Scolt Head Island and Minsmere, to shoot wildfowl in the marshes (with gun or camera, according to inclination), and above all for the sense of being away from it all that pours like a blessing from those vast East Anglian skies over flat coasts. Derelict buildings involved in abandoned or obsolete trades have been turned to other uses: Cley's windmill has been converted into a house, for example; Woodbridge tide mill now houses an exhibition, and its mill pond a yacht basin; the Maltings concert hall at Snape, near Aldeburgh, rings with music all year where a century ago barley was malted for the brewer; and small businesses have set up offices in Tollesbury's old wooden sail lofts.

The East London reaches of the Thames have seen great regeneration programmes at work along the lines of those at Liverpool's Albert Dock. The excellent shopping, entertainment, work and living accommodation at St Katharine's Dock and along the Wapping wharves is only a start. Acres of docks still lie out of use, choked with mud and ringed with derelict sites. City money is pumping new life into old veins and, simultaneously, pushing out an old, hard and close-knit community life that many locals are distressed to lose. Further along the river the disused end of Chatham dockyard, until recently the most impenetrable of fortresses, is now a splendid working museum.

SHERINGHAM, NORFOLK

In choking off the harbour lifelines of villages such as Wells, Blakeney and Cley, the sea dumps a tremendous amount of material from elsewhere. A good proportion of it comes from these cliffs that run south-east for many miles from Sheringham – cliffs made up of bands of chalk, clay and sand, soft and easily eroded. Winter waves crashing on these cliffs extract a heavy toll each year, and freshwater springs flowing inside the cliffs bring down more material, as do rainstorms. The beaches under the cliffs of north Norfolk are heaped with the litter of cliff falls. People living on this coastline soon get used to waking up after stormy nights to find that familiar stretches of road, footpaths, trees, hedges and even buildings have slipped over the cliff as they slept.

WAPPING PIER HEAD, LONDON

London's first proper docks were built here at the beginning of the nineteenth century. The cut leading off to the right of the picture was the original entrance to the docks, and the fine Georgian houses above it (here with Tower Bridge beyond) were built in 1811–13 for the dock officials, the dignity of their position reflected in the elegance of the architecture. Before the docks were built, Wapping was a notorious nest of rogues, a jumping-off point for pirates who would attack and rob passing ships on the river. There were more brothels and thieves' kitchens than respectable houses. The docks didn't put an end to that disreputable Wapping, but they regulated its activities. Nowadays the docks themselves are either derelict, or in the process of transformation into well-heeled playgrounds, their warehouses either demolished or converted into penthouses. But the vanished spice warehouses seem to have left behind them ghosts of smells – a whiff of cinnamon, a suspicion of cloves or pepper – still clinging to the places where they stood.

Meanwhile, the traditional livelihoods continue. Great Yarmouth and Lowestoft trawlers travel hundreds of miles after hundreds of tons of fish at one end of the scale; at the other, little wooden shellfish boats scour the Norfolk creeks for shrimps and mussels. Sadly, though, oysters have gone from most of the Essex creeks, wiped out by pollution, cold winters and disease; the industry has contracted around Mersea Island, where it hangs grimly on. The big town docks still bustle as the immense East Anglian grain prairies belch their harvest through the wharves and suck in fertilizers and pesticides, apparently insatiably. Some towns, like Great Yarmouth, have added North Sea oil rigs to their supply lists. Great Yarmouth has never been more popular, or successful, at wearing its other hat as a seaside resort. Located in a beautiful and often remote landscape, the East Anglian coastal settlements, big and small, seem set fair for a future at work and play as successful as, though utterly different from, their past glories.

KING'S LYNN, NORFOLK

King's Lynn – usually known simply as 'Lynn' – stands on the east bank of the River Great Ouse where it finally, slimily, reaches the sea in the marshes of the Wash. Lynn is full of beautiful buildings several hundred years old and strongly influenced by architectural fashions from across the North Sea. Dutch, Flemish and Scandinavian merchants all visited Lynn (and many settled here) in the Middle Ages, when the town was a valued member of the traders' Hanseatic League. In the centre of the picture stands the Customs House of 1683, topped by its white lantern tower and overshadowed by the enormous modern grain silos that spread a thick, yeasty smell over the riverside quarter of Lynn.

FISHER FLEET, KING'S LYNN, NORFOLK

The name of Fisher Fleet, a man-made inlet by the big docks north of Lynn's town centre, gives away its function. Here the little shrimp, cockle and mussel boats tie up, unload their catches and overhaul gear. A few of Lynn's shellfish boats are still of completely traditional design, clinker-built like *Renegade* in the photograph, though nowadays equipped with modern electronic aids for navigation and safety. The nature of fishing doesn't change, though: it's still long, wet and tiring work.

BRANCASTER STAITHE, NORFOLK

The Lynn mussel boat *Perseverance* lies up at Brancaster Staithe during a trip scouring the north Norfolk coastline's network of muddy creeks for shellfish. 'Staithe' means harbour hereabouts, and generations of fishermen have come to Brancaster Staithe on Mow Creek, in the shelter of Scolt Island, to mend nets, boil whelks and mussels, sit out storms or stretch their legs in a run ashore.

BLAKENEY, NORFOLK

As at Wells, huge amounts of sand surround Blakeney, where the great shingle bar of Blakeney Spit, four miles long at present, has been steadily growing westward since Norman times, adding inch by inch and year by year to the smothering collar of marsh, mud and sand around the seaward neck of Blakeney's River Glaven. Blakeney village may have lost its commercial port, but there are compensations: wonderful beaches, wildfowling in the marshes, sailing in the brackish reaches of Blakeney channel while sheltered by the shingle bar, and bird-watching in the National Trust's bird sanctuary at Blakeney Point on the western end of the spit.

ST NICHOLAS'S CHURCH, BLAKENEY, NORFOLK

St Nicholas is the patron saint of seafarers. When the church at Blakeney dedicated to him was being built in the fifteenth century, an extra tower was put up at the north-east corner for the guidance of those under his protection. A beacon lantern was kept burning in the chamber at the top, to help sailors and fishermen fix their positions at night. This secondary tower is 50ft high and only 8ft wide; the main tower at the western end is twice that height, and visible in the flat countryside as a landmark for miles around. The little upper window over the beautiful Early English chancel window next to the beacon tower is a rare feature in church architecture. It was put there to let light into a tiny chamber built in the space above the vaulted chancel ceiling. But none of the interior of St Nicholas's is dark – the clerestory windows high in the nave walls fill the church with that uniquely clear, liquid East Anglian light.

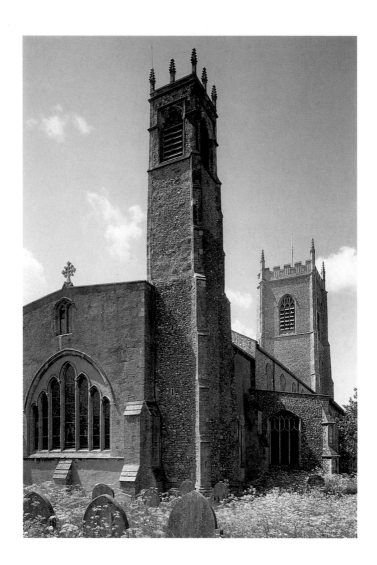

WIVETON, NORFOLK

The fifteenth-century church at Wiveton stands in lonely splendour above the flooded grassland that borders the River Glaven. Isolated on this watery stretch halfway between land and sea, the church tower once showed a guiding light to sailors; for these green meadows were a busy harbour in the Elizabethan and Stuart days when ships were built at Wiveton.

Silting would have killed Wiveton's port, as it did at Wells-next-the-Sea, without any human interference. But the natural process was accelerated when the local landowing family of Calthorpe built a great bank across the saltings in 1637 to drain the marsh of the Glaven estuary and reclaim it for farmland. Away went the water, the harbour and the trade. The bank was soon demolished, but there was no revival for Wiveton as the river silted up and the boggy acres spread.

CLEY NEXT THE SEA, NORFOLK

The red brick tower mill at Cley next the Sea (pronounced 'Cly') must be the most photographed and painted old windmill in Britain. Sited superbly over the salt marshes through which the River Glaven winds to the sea, the mill – all mills are feminine, like ships – still has her fantail, galleries and four great white sails on their 55ft stocks or crosspieces. She is dated 1713, but was probably completely rebuilt between that date and 1917 when she ceased grinding and entered a long period of use as a holiday house. In 1961 she was the first mill to be restored when Norfolk County Council decided to take in hand some of the county's hundreds of derelict mills. These days, looked after by the National Trust, she is used as a private dwelling, together with her cluster of flint cobble outbuildings.

CLEY NEXT THE SEA, NORFOLK

The old Customs House stands on the coast road, a stylish relic of Cley next the Sea's great days as a trading port. This fine brick building dates from the eighteenth century, but Cley rose to prosperity several hundred years earlier as a wool-then cloth-exporting centre.

The land reclamation schemes that cut off Wiveton from its trade did the same for Cley. The town, which had once been second in importance only to King's Lynn as a coastal port, shrank to an obscure backwater with a new and much reduced quay a mile nearer to the sea.

GREAT YARMOUTH, NORFOLK

Fine buildings line Hall Quay and South Quay on Great Yarmouth's waterfront, a tidal strip in the middle of town where three rivers mingle – the Yare, the Bure and the Waveney. Here the influences of Low Countries architecture have crept in among and enriched the home-grown variety. Great Yarmouth grew sleekly prosperous on its fame as Britain's premier herring-fishing and curing port. Yarmouth Bloaters – herrings smoked just so – are still a delicacy to be savoured. But after the Second World War the great herring shoals quit the east coast waters, leaving behind strong memories in Great Yarmouth. As Norfolk's most popular seaside resort, however, Great Yarmouth (that part of the town that faces away from the waterfront and on to the North Sea) goes from strength to strength – every East Anglian's number one choice for a lively week in a lovely resort.

THE FISHERMEN'S HOSPITAL, GREAT YARMOUTH, NORFOLK

Built in 1702 on Church Plain just near the Church of St Nicholas, the Fishermen's Hospital was founded by the town's Corporation to provide almshouse accommodation for about thirty 'decayed fishermen' who had reached the age of sixty. Each tiny cottage had its dormer window and looked out on to the statue of Charity in the centre of the cobbled courtyard, while St Peter – no mean fisherman himself – looked benevolently down from the cupola. Restored several times already this century, the original thirty or so cottages have been combined into about fifteen, each twice the size. The trust that now administers the Fishermen's Hospital has kept its original purpose: elderly fishermen and their wives still live here.

LOWESTOFT, SUFFOLK

Fishing made Lowestoft's fortune back in the sixteenth century, and fishing has remained the mainstay of the town. When the east coast curse of a silted harbour threatened Lowestoft's livelihood in the 1840s, Sir Samuel Peto stepped in to have it enlarged, improved, unsilted and supplied with a railway line. Today it has a busy fish market (gull shrieks are a source of serious noise pollution here), boat-building yards, and a fleet of trawlers that go out on ten-day expeditions as near Iceland as they dare go. The boats sacrifice picturesqueness to practicality. Everything on board is functional, even down to the lurid orange paint that helps them to be seen by air-sea rescue crews. An old-time Lowestoft fisherman would be baffled by the sophistication of the operation, though. Sonic fish-finding equipment lets the skipper know when and where to look for fish, how to get there, what kind of fish they are and their speed, depth and direction.

SNAPE MALTINGS, SUFFOLK

For hundreds of years barley malted here in Snape Maltings was carried out along the many muddy miles of the winding Rivers Alde and Ore to the sea in Hollesley Bay, and thence to the ever-thirsty breweries. But that long journey downriver began to look too time-consuming once the roads had improved and the railway arrived to whisk the malted barley away to its destination in a fraction of the time. The Maltings quay at Snape declined and closed, not to re-awaken until a Lowestoft dentist's son began to fill the echoing old buildings with music. Benjamin Britten's concert hall, constructed inside one of the maltings buildings, soon became the hub of the annual Aldeburgh Festival of Music. On the first night of the 1969 season the concert hall caught fire and was destroyed, but feverish work saw it ready for the opening of the following year's Festival.

ORFORD, SUFFOLK

The evening tide recedes from Cuckold's Point, whose muddy flanks lead the eye northwards over the River Alde towards Orford Castle and the church of St Bartholomew. The castle, built in 1165–6 at about the same date as the church, has a cylindrical centre and three square towers, much clambered over, sketched and besieged by visiting school parties. Orford village is a quiet haven nowadays, with several good pubs and miles of windy, marshy walking country. At one time the village had a thriving harbour, but it was silted out of existence as the great shingle bank of Orfordness lengthened out south-west from Orford. Originating in pebble deposits brought by the rising seas at the end of the last Ice Age, Orfordness now runs six miles from Orford, shepherding the River Alde, or Ore, along an ever-lengthening channel before it at last reaches the sea.

WOODBRIDGE, SUFFOLK

Woodbridge has been called 'the most unspoilt small town in Suffolk', an opinion it's hard to disagree with once one is sauntering among its narrow streets of old brick and flint houses, well shaded by trees. Where the River Deben reaches the town ten miles inland, the yachts ride peacefully against the wharves once piled with tiles, coal, heaps of grain and stacks of timber. Woodbridge's tide mill stands at the heart of this former hive of activity, on the oldest site of any tide mill in Britain – occupied since before 1200. The mill worked on simple but effective principles. The incoming tide forced its way through gates to fill the mill pond. As the tide turned, its outgoing pressure squeezed the gates shut from inside, trapping the water in the pond. Other gates then opened, and the water rushed out along a channel to turn the 20ft diameter mill wheel. The red-roofed mill was built in the eighteenth century.

IPSWICH, SUFFOLK

A sailing barge spreads her great brown sails beautifully against the grain palaces of St Peter's Quay on the River Orwell in Ipswich – a quay better known to locals as the Wet Dock. The Thames Barges that grace the Orwell today are the lovingly maintained remnants of a vast coasting fleet that plied between Ipswich and London until after the Second World War. Before Suffolk barley, it was Suffolk woollen cloth that jingled the moneybags of Ipswich. Today's cargoes that pass through the Wet Dock include roadstone from Teesside, steel from the Common Market, and logs going out to Scandinavia – coals to Newcastle, one might think. The mills that stand along the quay no longer receive their corn by water, but by road. Yachts, Thames Barges and the occasional visiting tall ship, however, still keep life and colour on the Orwell.

PIN MILL, SUFFOLK

South and east from Ipswich runs the unfrequented Shotley peninsula, bounded on the north by the River Orwell and on the south by the River Stour. Pin Mill, facing the Orwell on the northern shore of the peninsula, lies down a narrow lane on a muddy foreshore and boasts a few small cottages, a chandler's store, a collection of old barges and one of the best and most atmospheric pubs in England, the Butt and Oyster, which at high tide stands with its outer wall in the river. Arthur Ransome often sailed from Pin Mill, and so did his 'Swallows' in *We Didn't Mean To Go To Sea* and *Secret Water*. Ransome would recognize those who sail there today: still the same informal, gumbooted family outings in tiny sailing dinghies. In his opinion – and in mine, fifty years on – Pin Mill is one of the most delightful spots on earth.

WIVENHOE, ESSEX

Evening sun brushes golden light across the quayside at Wivenhoe, a boat-building and sailing haven a couple of miles south of Colchester on the muddy banks of the River Colne. This is a lovely spot to sit outside one of the waterfront pubs on a fine summer evening, dangling your legs above the tide and sniffing in that marshy smell of the Essex coastline – warm vegetation, salt, wood varnish and tidal river water.

TOLLESBURY, ESSEX

Tollesbury, a little town on the remote salt marshes that fringe the northern side of the River Blackwater, has been a centre for amateur sailors since Victorian days. The enormous sails of the great 'J' or Jumbo class racing yachts of the early years of this century were dried off and stored in these wooden sail lofts, built in 1902, at Tollesbury's harbour. The 'J's have vanished from the seas, but their sail lofts continue to be used. They are full of little business premises and offices: an architect, a yacht charter firm, the office of Christian Fellowship Afloat. The interiors have been scrupulously cleaned and decorated – a far cry from their previous use.

MALDON, ESSEX

The wide Blackwater Estuary begins to narrow as it curls past Hythe quay and the church of St Mary the Virgin towards the ancient town of Maldon. Here the pleasure boats lie up on the gravel, often joined by restored Thames Barges. Maldon sea salt, made in the town, is famous for its tart pungency. Senior citizens of Maldon remember the days when the Blackwater estuary was so thickly grown with weed that it could be hard to find a passage at low tide. These days, pollution from the sewer of Europe, the North Sea, has almost wiped out the Blackwater weed, leaving the estuary, ironically, a better place for sailing.

BURNHAM-ON-CROUCH, ESSEX

Below the Blackwater estuary lies the large, blunt-nosed Dengie peninsula. Unvisited by tourists, it is Essex at its most bleak and haunting. On the southern side of the peninsula, washed by the murky waters of the River Crouch, is Burnham-on-Crouch, a little town with a long history of passing trade. Medieval pilgrims from Europe, on their way to Norfolk and the Shrine of Our Lady at Walsingham, would disembark here; and inhabitants of the many remote, flat islands of the outer Thames estuary would ferry themselves across to Burnham for supplies.

Burnham has become a noted yachting centre, its river crowded with sails and its pubs with sailors. Londoners escape here for weekends. As at Wivenhoe, the smells of salt, tar and marine varnish are never far away.

HADLEIGH CASTLE, ESSEX

The massive ruins of Hadleigh Castle stand on the northern bank of the River Thames, looking out over the flat wastes of Canvey Island (with its oil, gas and aviation fuel storage, a time-bomb waiting to go up) to the wide throat of the Thames and the low hills of the Kentish shore. Hadleigh Castle's towers have walls 9ft thick. When the castle was rebuilt in the 1360s on the site of an earlier Norman fortification, on the orders of King Edward III, the Hundred Years War with the French was just in its infancy and the king feared an invasion up the Thames. It never happened, but Hadleigh Castle found a role as a makeweight in the dowries of several queens – Henry VIII gave it to three of his wives. Most of the castle was destroyed in a landslide, but Turner found the ruins striking enough to paint in 1828. Their sombre emptiness chimed with his mood, for Turner had just lost his dearly loved wife.

GREENWICH, LONDON

Wide bends of the River Thames at Greenwich gleam in the distance beyond the graceful outline of the National Maritime Museum, housed together with the Royal Naval College on the site of the Tudor monarchs' country retreat, the Palace of Placentia.

This view over the green spaces of Greenwich Park is from the buildings of the old Royal Observatory, founded in 1675 and now a museum. When London smogs became too thick for even the instruments of the Royal Observatory to penetrate, it shifted operations after World War II to Herstmonceux Castle in Sussex.

ST KATHARINE'S DOCK, TOWER HAMLETS, LONDON

Over St Katharine's Dock stands the Ivory House, a colonnaded warehouse built in 1854 to store ivory from Britain's African colonies. By the 1960s all the warehouses around St Katharine's Dock, which was built between 1824 and 1828 by Thomas Telford, were semi-derelict, the dock itself falling into disuse. Now the whole place has been smartened up with a yacht marina, a floating museum of sailing vessels, designer shops and pubs, excellent restaurants, exclusive flats. It's all part of the regeneration of London's dockland, long overdue but viewed with some cynicism by East Enders who see their dock-related traditions and atmosphere replaced by something a good deal less highly spiced, if also more salubrious.

ROCHESTER, KENT

The city of Rochester lies on the east bank of the River Medway, where it begins to thread towards its meeting with the Thames between the Isles of Grain and Sheppey. Charles Dickens knew the city well, and featured it in many of his books – *Pickwick Papers*, *Great Expectations* and *The Mystery of Edwin Drood*, among others.

A Celtic community lived on Rochester's site, the Romans founded their town of Durobrivae here, and an Anglo-Saxon settlement followed. William the Conqueror had a castle built here, though the great 113ft keep seen in the photograph belongs to its successor, built in the late 1120s. The reason for such importance attaching for so long to this site by the Medway? Rochester commands what for two thousand years has been the chief river crossing between London and Canterbury, the Kent country and the Channel ports, and a lot of river traffic still uses the Medway here.

CHATHAM, KENT

The dockyard that King Henry VIII established at Chatham grew over the next four hundred years into a labyrinth of 20-acre repair basins, construction slips and workshops. Nelson's flagship *Victory* was built here, along with many other famous ships. Now, while the northern or Victorian end of the site is still ticking over, repairing ships and refitting nuclear submarines, the whole of the southern or Georgian end has been opened by the Historic Dockyard Trust as a working museum. The photograph shows No 3 Slip, opened in 1838, the oldest ship construction slip at Chatham and probably the oldest covered slip in the world. The slip was built of wood by skilled shipwrights, and the influence of their usual work is shown clearly when you stand inside this tall, barn-like building and look up to the cross-beams of the roof: it's exactly like standing in the belly of an upturned ship.

SITTINGBOURNE, KENT

Sittingbourne also has a shipyard museum, but a rather different one from Chatham's echoing acres of concrete, stone and brick. At the Dolphin Sailing Barge Museum in Crown Quay Lane on Bourne Creek, you can watch the old Thames Barges being restored – spritsail barges are the staple diet – before wandering around the museum's exhibitions of shipbuilding, shipwrights' tools, models and paintings of barges. It is one of the few examples along the English coastline of a boatyard in better shape now than it has ever been.

FAVERSHAM, KENT

From Faversham, a pretty, small town stuffed with buildings from the last five hundred years, Faversham Creek runs north to meet the Swale and then the Thames. The creek is still busy with sailing boats, but during the last century it was an important trading waterway. In 1862 this imposing storehouse (the 'Big Building' to local people) was built beside the creek by the Chambers family of brickmakers, barge owners and dealers in hay, straw and corn. In recent years, as the half-decipherable legends on its wall show, it has done duty as the boat-building premises of the Oyster Bay Ship Yard Company, and the storage barn of United Fertiliser. Today, not old or historic enough to be granted listed building status, the Big Building sits empty and silent by the creek, waiting either for demolition or for someone's inspiration to spark it into life again.

WHITSTABLE, KENT

Whitstable, on the Kentish shore of the Thames Estuary, has been oyster-orientated since Roman times. Oysters thrive in its particular environment of salt and fresh water, temperature and algal food. Julius Caesar failed to find the pearls he'd hoped for, but his followers discovered something else to enthuse over inside those wrinkled shells. Today you can still buy 'Royal Natives' in Whitstable: they are said to taste of nothing much, but in a heavenly manner.

Whitstable's harbour is a busy place: gravel is imported here, coasters put in with a variety of cargoes, and in the tall black sheds on the quay the shell-fishermen boil up their catches of cockles and whelks. The harbour has a niche in history, for it was the first one in the world to have its own steam railway, built to connect Whitstable with Canterbury back in 1830.

The South Coast

A row of old coastguard cottages looks out across Cuckmere Haven to the chalk cliffs of the Seven Sisters marching away east towards Beachy Head. The cottages were built as part of the never-ending struggle of the excisemen against the eighteenth-century Sussex smugglers, who were based at Alfriston just up the valley and always seemed to keep their illicit brandy, tobacco and lace one jump ahead of the King's Men. These days such excitements are unknown at Cuckmere Haven, one of the most peaceful spots along the south coast in its new role as the Seaford Haven Nature Reserve. The reserve protects three entirely different kinds of habitat in one small area – wet pasture, foreshore and the Sussex downland that stretched all along these cliffs until Second World War ploughing decimated it.

*T*he English face their favourite traditional enemy, the French, over the busiest waterway in the world. The ports and harbours of England's south coast perfectly reflect the split in the national personality of this island people – garrison-minded defence alongside eager wanderlust. Under attack or threat of attack throughout the centuries, this coastline is studded with forts, castles, ditches, walls, gun emplacements and look-out towers defending its business of moving people and goods into, out of and around the country. Forts against the French in Tudor times, ditch barriers against the invasion troops of Napoleon, ugly concrete pill-boxes against those of Hitler – no matter during which century or for which emergency they were constructed, very few of these coastal defences ever saw a shot fired in anger. The invasion threat has been a constant and very real one, however: Danes raided the pre-Norman Isle of Thanet; the Normans won that little set-to near Hastings; the Spanish Armada was blown and harried the whole length of the south coast; Napoleon's invasion troops were aimed at Romney Marsh; great swathes of Southampton and Portsmouth were bombed flat during the Second World War.

At a time of great trouble with French looting and arson raids in the thirteenth century, Hastings and Dover had cause to bless the wisdom of Edward the Confessor, who had overseen their banding together with Romney, Hythe and Sandwich in the Cinque Ports confederacy. They guarded each others' backs, they all contributed to the fleet that did battle with the French whenever necessary, and they all profited hugely from the perks and privileges that were their reward for this coastal defence duty. Rye, however, having joined the confederacy in the twelfth century, found out in 1377 what the French could do when they *did* get ashore: they burned the town to cinders. Rye's neighbour, Winchelsea, was the other latecomer to the Cinque Ports club, and both towns, together with Romney, were eventually stranded high and dry by silting and storms. Silting has affected some river ports, and shingle drift some harbours along the south coast, but less catastrophically than on the crumbly eastern coast of England.

While attack threatened, of course, the south coast ports and harbours were also doing some pretty nifty attacking and raiding themselves, as well as sending out fleets and expeditions to all parts of the world. Southampton has spun out this thread of tradition for close on a thousand years, from Crusades to Cunarders by way of military expeditions to France, New World settlers' voyages, Napoleonic Wars troopships and Canadian emigration steamers. Once pleasure travel abroad became the rage, a line of Channel ports – Dover, Folkstone, Newhaven, Weymouth – stretched across to grab the Continental trade. And fishing, as it did everywhere round the English coast, sustained a basic economy in seaside settlements large and small, those at the eastern end of the Channel extending their fishing grounds out into the southern part of the North Sea, those at the western end looking towards the Atlantic. Where fishing throve, so did smuggling. Caves in the chalk and sandstone cliffs, hideouts in the wastes of Romney Marsh, barns and cellars in the inland Sussex towns, all gave excisemen continual headaches, and local people some fun and profit.

The biggest visible stamp on the south coast communities has undoubtedly been set by generations of holidaymakers and health-seekers. You won't find better examples of Regency terraces, squares and crescents than on the clifftops and waterfront parades of Ramsgate, Brighton, Hove or Weymouth; while the hotels and boarding houses, restaurants and dance halls, gift shops and car parks, caravans and mobile homes have multiplied in the last two hundred years to fill up almost every gap between the houses right the way along the whole of the Sussex coastline, from Seaford almost to Portsmouth – a good sixty miles. The leisure industry has brought a prosperity to the south coast that those dusty coal ports of the north-east coast and the faded ore harbours of Cumbria can only envy. Small places cash in as readily as big ones; an afternoon in the cobbled, hilly streets of red-roofed Rye, or an evening watching the boats go by on Bosham's waterfront, are as attractive to some visitors as the amusement arcades of Brighton or the space-invader palaces of Bournemouth are to others. Good sailing spots are like gold dust, too. Weekend sailors flock to the south coast's natural harbours of Chichester, Christchurch and Poole.

Some of the large resorts have not been in touch with their original roots as fishing harbours or coasting ports for a very long time, and have moved unimaginably far from the kind of fish-stinking, iron-clanking practicality of such places. But their

DEAL CASTLE, KENT

When France and Spain signed a non-aggression pact in 1539, King Henry VIII immediately saw it as an anti-English move, conveying an imminent threat of war and invasion. He ordered a line of forts to be strung round England's southern coastline, of which Deal was the first and most interestingly structured, and remains the best preserved. Deal Castle was built in 1540 to command The Downs, the excellent deep-water anchorage in the roadstead between the Kent coast and the Goodwin Sands. The castle is shaped like a Tudor rose, an outer moat enclosing six semi-circular bastions, which in turn enclose six more, which in their turn enclose a central tower. The varying heights of the bastions meant that three levels of artillery – 145 gun embrasures altogether – could be brought to bear at the same time. The castle's harmoniously flowing shape proved to be the best thing about it, however, as during the Civil War it failed to withstand a Roundhead siege.

WEYMOUTH, DORSET

Weymouth harbour is one of Dorset's narrow-mouthed havens. A mile north of here the River Wey flows into Radipole Lake, known in times past as the Backwater and a great spot for stick-and-pin-style fishing. An important medieval wool port that experienced re-birth as a select Georgian resort, Weymouth does two sorts of business: one with the town's steady band of faithful yearly holidaymakers (a bit of sun, a bit of fun), the other with the Channel Islands as a ferry port and receiving station for the islands' produce of fruit and vegetables, including the famous tomatoes.

industry, frivolous though it may appear, is as solid an economy — more solid, nowadays — as any traditional industrial working base of ports like Dover, Shoreham, Portsmouth and Southampton. Further west, some places like Poole and Weymouth carry on trade and tourism side by side.

Change is attacking the south coast as vigorously as the other coasts of England. When that hole in the ground near Folkstone becomes the Eurotunnel rail link with France under the Channel, the town of Folkestone can expect to benefit enormously. Most of Folkstone's ferrymen, however, will probably be out of a job — as will those at Dover, just along the coast. These people see change as a threat to their communities, something to be feared. So do local people contemplating the expensive new marinas and 'exclusive waterside villages' being proposed by sharp development companies for the harbours and quays of many a south coast town. They want to know who will really benefit from schemes like these; the answers they get don't satisfy them. Then there are expansion plans for villages, and threats to develop what to planners appear muddy bogs, but to conservationists are havens for rare wildlife.

But change has always been endemic along the south coast. This, after all, was the coast where Brighthelmstone fishing village swelled into mighty Brighton, where a great shipbuilding industry grew from nothing into a giant and dwindled back to nothing again at Buckler's Hard, and where a king's illness changed Weymouth in a few years from an obscure port down on its luck into a watering place at the forefront of fashion. If any coast can cope with change, it's this one.

BROADSTAIRS, KENT

Broadstairs beach is as well-behaved and suitable as you can imagine, glimpsed between boats at the jetty; but thereby hangs a tale of most un-Broadstairs-like moral turpitude. In 1969 a great wooden marina broke away from its moorings on the French coast in a February storm, and floated across the Channel into Joss Bay a mile or two north of Broadstairs. All locals, including the papers, were sworn to secrecy until a month was up, after which time the French owners of the runaway marina lost the right to reclaim it. The marina just nicely filled in some gaps in Broadstairs's old jetty.

You can just imagine this story woven into brilliant colour by Charles Dickens, who often visited Broadstairs between 1836 and 1850, some of his most fruitful writing years. Above the harbour stands the castellated house where Dickens frequently stayed, and where he finished writing *David Copperfield*.

RAMSGATE, KENT

Regency terraces and crescents on the cliffs of Ramsgate make the view inland from the harbour walls one of the most striking in England. Albion House, at the seaward end of the elegant white terrace in the middle distance, played host to Queen Victoria when she came to Ramsgate as a young girl; and Mrs Fitzherbert stayed at Albion Place next door between 1797 and 1799, waiting to be summoned back to Brighton by George, Prince of Wales, whose wife was giving him partly merited hell. Jane Austen stayed there a few years later, and many Ramsgate scenes appear in *Pride and Prejudice*. But if the developers get their way, this historic view will be obscured by expensive apartment blocks rising above a new marina in Ramsgate harbour. 'Jobs and prestige for a fading resort' say those in favour. 'Rich outsiders changing our views to suit their whims' reply those against. Which will talk louder – money, or local feeling? Watch that space.

DOVER, KENT

A rusty old three-master lies at ease among the impudent yachts and dinghies in the inner harbour at Dover. The town still clangs and shouts with sea activity and sea talk, as the cross-Channel ferries and freighters arrive and depart. Dover Castle surveys it all from nearly 500ft up, as it has done for eight centuries.

Dover came through some terrible bombing and shelling in both world wars with its spirit undented, but a more subtle enemy to this ferryport, and one greatly feared by Dover dock workers, is slowly shaping up a few miles to the west – a swift, smooth and secure railway route under the sea through the Channel Tunnel. When that opens in 1993, Dover ferries may soon be as obsolete as the three-master.

FOLKESTONE, KENT

It is Folkestone that is poised to be the beneficiary of the soon-to-be-opened Channel Tunnel, though here, too, the ferry workers would not agree with this assessment. The tunnel terminal will be nearby, and millions of visitors and business men and women, as well as millions of tons of freight, are expected to flood both ways. Prosperity from the railway is nothing new in Folkestone's experience. When the trains first arrived in 1842 the town quickly mushroomed into a most desirable Victorian seaside resort. Echoes of that less flustered era can be caught at the little shellfish stalls around the harbour. Here for a few pence you can get a handful of vinegary, salty cockles or whelks to chew as you idle along by the harbour railings, over which the trawler nets are draped to dry.

RYE, SUSSEX

Mud, mud, glorious mud covers the banks of the River Rother, which brought enormous prosperity to Rye when the Great Storm of 1287 wrenched its flow into a new course at the foot of the ancient Sussex town. Such prosperity, in fact, that Rye became a member of the Cinque Ports trading and defence confederacy, and flourished for a couple of hundred years. But nature had been gradually stealing away the sweets that she had so fortunately bestowed on Rye. Silt blocked off the sea channel, and the town, finding itself stranded three miles inland, turned to local trading, fishing and smuggling for its living.

RYE, SUSSEX

From the top of St Mary's Church tower the view to the north-east looks across Rye's red roofs and charming, tightly twisting streets, where Henry James came to live in 1890 and remained until his death in 1916. He lived at Lamb House in West Street, later the home of E. F. Benson, author of the 'Lucia' novels and Mayor of Rye from 1934 to 1937. In the distance lie the level green pastures of Walland Marsh, which abuts the great flat saucer of Romney Marsh – seventy or eighty square miles of some of the most fertile land in Britain. It was reclaimed from the sea by the medieval monks after the Romans had made a start with a sea wall at Dymchurch. In Roman days, when the River Rother ran in its pre-1287 course, Romney Marsh was a wide bay full of small islands. The blue line of today's South Downs escarpment, seen on the horizon at the far right of the photograph, was then a line of cliffs dropping into the sea.

HASTINGS, SUSSEX

On the beach at Hastings known as the Stade lie the town's fishing boats, waiting for the next tide. Hastings once boasted a fleet of over a hundred boats, but silt strangled the old harbour that had brought prosperity to the town through membership of the Cinque Ports confederacy. A grand new one, planned in the 1890s to replace it, was never finished – a crumbling arm of it can be seen behind the boats. Now the fishermen just pull straight up on to the beach. Final indignity – they are all registered RX, for Rye.

HASTINGS, SUSSEX

Called 'tackle-boxes', 'net-shops' or 'deezes', the net lofts of Hastings, some of them three storeys high and a few as much as three hundred years old, are a tourist attraction these days. The fishermen built them thin to pay as little ground rent as possible, and tall to get all the gear in. The tar weatherproofing of yesteryear has largely given way to creosote, but Hastings fishermen can still be seen sitting and mending nets outside their net lofts.

NEWHAVEN, SUSSEX

The Newhaven-Dieppe ferry leaves Newhaven Harbour in a flat calm. It was a great storm, however, which blew Newhaven some good in 1759 by forcing the River Ouse three miles out of its course, from Seaford in the east to a new outfall below the village of Meeching. The 'new haven', once formed, did what all English harbours love to do – it silted up. But the 2,400ft West Pier, built in the nineteenth century, solved that. The Newhaven-Dieppe ferry service was inaugurated in 1843, and still does the 72-mile run in a little over three hours – if conditions are like those pictured here.

WEST PIER, NEWHAVEN, SUSSEX

This little wood-slatted light-hut was built in the late nineteenth century in the Newhaven Harbour marine workshops on the eastern side of the harbour, and positioned at the narrowest part of the West Pier to show a light to ships. To transport the hut nearly two miles from workshops to West Pier, a narrow-gauge railway was laid, and the hut, fitted with wheels, was trundled to its resting place. No-one bothered to remove the wheels or the length of rail under the hut, so they are still there today. The hut is still in use, burning a green light, though powered by electricity in place of the original oil.

SHOREHAM, SUSSEX

Though you would never suspect it from this tranquil aspect looking across the River Adur, Shoreham has a shoreline thronged with docks, wharves and jetties for oil, timber and container vessels. In medieval times it was the busiest port on this coast, but nature changed all that. By the end of the fourteenth century the sea had eaten all of shoreline Shoreham, and a shingle spit growing along the coast pushed the mouth of the Adur parallel to the shore for mile after mile, further and further east. Trade was in a bad way until a new exit for the river was cut halfway along the shingle bank. The rivers of this shingly, chalky coastline have always been prone to moves and shifts of position and condition. Before the Romans ever came to Sussex, the Adur spread in a wide estuary, perhaps as far as five miles inland.

BOSHAM, SUSSEX

'The sea creek, the green field, the grey church' wrote Tennyson of Bosham (pronounced 'Bozz'm'), a concise summing-up of the peaceful attractions of this quiet corner of Chichester Harbour. Sailors love it: so much so, that Bosham is best visited well out of season. In spite of narrow streets of brick and flint cottages, marshland smells and sounds, and the superb Church of the Holy Trinity (the tower base is Saxon, as is the chancel arch, founded on two Roman stones), Bosham has avoided the worst of dimity tourist charm.

Early visitors were the Danes, who took away a souvenir in the form of the church bell. The monks of Bosham, who rang the remaining bells as the Danes were heading out of the harbour, in thanksgiving at not having been put to the sword, heard the stolen bell responding and watched it vibrating with increasing force until it slipped off the marauders' deck and sank to the bed of the harbour.

BIRTHPLACE OF CHARLES DICKENS, PORTSMOUTH, HAMPSHIRE

Charles Dickens was born in 1812 in this modest brick house, which was then 387 Mile End Terrace, Commercial Road, Portsea. Charles's father, John Dickens, worked as a Naval Pay Office clerk in the Portsmouth dockyard before a stint at Chatham. Six months after Charles's birth the family moved to a smaller house – John Dickens was often in financial difficulties – before moving away to London in 1814. In 1901 the street was renumbered, and 387 Mile End Terrace became 393 Commercial Road. The house is now the Dickens Museum, full of Dickens memorabilia and open every day.

PORTSMOUTH, HAMPSHIRE

The Royal Naval dockyard at Portsmouth has enough famous connections to sink a battleship. The first dock here was ordered in 1194 by King Richard the Lionheart, and in 1495 King Henry VII caused the world's first dry dock to be built at Portsmouth. During the Napoleonic Wars Portsmouth became the heart of the Royal Navy, always ready to serve the sailors. During the Second World War a good deal of Portsmouth was knocked flat in bombing raids, but the dockyards went on operating. For the Royal Navy, entering the Spithead roadstead that leads to the dockyard at 'Pompey' is like turning into your own front drive. Today the Royal Naval dockyard plays host to England's most famous ship, *HMS Victory*, Nelson's flagship, which, now completely restored, is in her own dry dock after years afloat in the harbour.

BARGATE, SOUTHAMPTON, HAMPSHIRE

Sited on a peninsula tip, Southampton has always been vulnerable to attack from nearly all points of the compass. In Norman times the town was completely surrounded with defensive walls (more than half of which still stand today), guarded by towers with lovely names – Polymond, God's House Tower, Windwhistle and Catchcold – and pierced by great fortified gates. Bargate, seen here bathed in early evening sunlight, is the northern gate of the old town, its flanking drum towers dating from the thirteenth century. In 1400 Southampton's Guildhall (now a museum) was established in the upper storey of Bargate, and in the same century the top of the gate was crowned with its castellated parapet. The lions on their pedestals were cast in lead and placed on guard outside Bargate in 1743.

SOUTHAMPTON, HAMPSHIRE

One of the most vigorous scenes along the south coast is the Southampton waterfront, seen here from the River Itchen as it broadens out to meet the River Test at their confluence at the head of Southampton Water. Crusaders embarked at Southampton; so did troops for the Hundred Years War; so did the Pilgrim Fathers aboard *Mayflower* and *Speedwell* in 1620, and soldiers bound for Waterloo. In 1842 the first docks opened, and Southampton developed into an unrivalled passenger port. Bombing raids in 1940–41 tore much of the town to pieces, but it was able to muster the back-up for the D-Day embarkation of tens of thousands of troops.

Those pre-war passenger liner glory days have departed, and Southampton has now become an important commercial centre, but it still draws a good deal of its pride, if not quite as much sustenance, from its docks and waterfront.

BUCKLER'S HARD, HAMPSHIRE

At first sight it's hard to fathom why two terraces of red brick cottages should have been built on either side of an abnormally wide main street along an otherwise deserted stretch of the beautiful Beaulieu River, at the foot of Southampton Water. The functional, skeletal frameworks seen here give a clue: they are sheer-legs, for lifting heavy boat-building materials. Two hundred years ago, Buckler's Hard was famous for shipbuilding and employed four thousand men and a covey of skilled shipwrights in building ships-of-the-line for Nelson's navy. Its wide street was used for seasoning stacks of oak timbers from the nearby New Forest. By 1840 the boom was over, though during the Second World War business returned to Buckler's Hard in the shape of orders for wood-hulled ships unattractive to magnetic mines. A maritime museum now flourishes in the village.

MUDEFORD, DORSET

Christchurch Harbour is an almost enclosed bowl of water formed by the flowing together of the Stour and Avon rivers on the eastern outskirts of Bournemouth. This view looks from Hengistbury Head across the narrow jaws of the harbour, only a few yards wide and known as the Avon Run, to the former fishing village (now mostly a yachting haven) of Mudeford, where old pubs and cottages, their walls traditionally tarred against the weather, stand attractively by the harbour mouth. A little pot fishing and some winter and spring salmon netting still keep the tang of fish wafting faintly around Mudeford.

CHRISTCHURCH, DORSET

Christchurch Priory rises above the trees on the north bank of the River Stour. The church was begun soon after the Norman Conquest, and in 1150 was taken over by the Augustinian priory that established itself here. The monks finally finished the body of the church a century later, and added its 120ft tower about a hundred and fifty years after that. It was a slow gestation, and a faulty conception, too. According to legend, the original site for the church was planned to be on St Catherine's Hill, three miles further inland. Every morning the builders would arrive on site at the top of the hill, to find that the previous day's work had been mysteriously dismantled and removed downriver to the peninsula site where the Stour and Avon met. But it was not until one of the roof beams, which had been cut too short, was miraculously lengthened that the builders moved site and built with no more trouble.

POOLE HARBOUR, DORSET

What Christchurch Harbour is in miniature, Poole Harbour is writ large. Only about five miles from east to west, less than that from north to south, the harbour is so indented with creeks, inlets and stream mouths that its shoreline stretches for close to a hundred miles. It's a tremendous natural harbour, one of the largest in the world, its shores an intriguing mixture of port and wharf development in the north at Poole, and almost untouched heath, bog and scrub everywhere else. And Poole Harbour gets twice as many high tides as other places. No one knows exactly why – it has something to do with the shape of the harbour, something to do with the way the Isle of Wight obstructs the English Channel. Ships of all sizes have to squeeze in and out of an extremely narrow entrance between Sandbanks and South Haven Point. Hence the Harbour Authority tugs, without which the big ships could not operate.

LULWORTH COVE, DORSET

Lulworth Cove, the most famous (and most visited) cove on the Dorset coast, is best enjoyed out of season, preferably when a good gale is blowing, to watch the sea at its demolition work. The strata of the cliffs, of oolitic Portland limestone, were buckled and bent by enormous volcanic movements of the earth's crust hundreds of millions of years ago. In such twisted rock plates are weaknesses, one of which the sea eventually broke through to reach and demolish the softer beds of clay behind. At the back of those lies chalk, which the waves are now getting to work on, scooping away at the bowl-shaped cove – a hard horseshoe of rock enfolding softer material, which slowly, inexorably, washes away as the storms of millennia each dig a little deeper than the last.

PORTLAND BILL, DORSET

The Isle of Portland – 'The Gibraltar of Wessex' – slants into the Channel off the underside of Weymouth. Grey, angular, quarried into a pockmarked honeycomb, treeless, windswept and topped by a Borstal and a prison, it's not exactly a paradise island, but it is powerfully atmospheric. The cliffs of Portland slope the full four-mile length of the island, from nearly 500ft at the northern end down to 20ft at Portland Bill, the southernmost tip marked by the white-painted obelisk seen in the photograph. A couple of old lighthouses stand here near the red-and-white striped 136ft tower of the current one, opened in 1906. Its light is of three million candlepower and is visible eighteen miles away. It needs to be, for off Portland Bill writhes and clashes one of the most powerful tide rips in Britain.

LYME REGIS, DORSET

Scores of small boats ride easy in the harbour at Lyme Regis, the best haven for many miles, sheltered as it is by the curving, fossil-studded breakwater of the massive Cobb, seven centuries old, from whose broad, sloping back this photograph was taken. The main part of the little town, made famous by Jane Austen in *Persuasion* and, a century and a half later, by John Fowles in *The French Lieutenant's Woman*, lies a good half mile east of the Cobb. The cliff behind the town is Black Ven, under whose shaky flanks Mary Anning helped her brother to dig out the first fossil Ichthyosaurus to be discovered. Black Ven and the other cliffs of this coastline, sandwiches of unstable clays, chalk and rocks, are slipping – not so slowly, and sometimes with dramatic suddenness – into the sea. This picture clearly shows the greensand top of the cliff (golden in colour), exposed by recent falls, and the grey-black skirt of crumbling Blue Lias below, in which fossils are found.

SIDMOUTH, DEVON

Sidmouth is another resort with strong literary connections. Jane Austen, holidaying here with her parents in 1801, lost her heart to a handsome young man, who promptly died, leaving Jane with a dolorous wound whose effects lasted her lifetime. Elegant Regency architecture and some fancy associations – King George III, Queen Victoria, Grand Duchess Hélène of Russia, Lord Despenser the 'notorious libertine' – have graced (or lumbered) Sidmouth with the title 'The Aristocrat of the East Devon Coast'. But side by side with all this nineteenth-century frippery went Sidmouth's other life as a working fishing town. The medieval harbour had silted up; the one planned in the 1830s, according to local accounts, was abandoned when the railway engine provided to shift the construction stone along the shore was found to be too big to get through the tunnel that had been built for it.

EXMOUTH, DEVON

Several miles south of Exeter, on the east bank of the River Exe where it meets the sea, Exmouth is prized for its clean, yellow sands and family resort atmosphere. A dock opened at Exmouth in 1871, and for a while was very busy; but the Exe was slowly silting then, and still is. All those sands, such good news for holidaymaking families, are less welcome to the town's mackerel fishermen who have to beach their boats in a drying estuary. But for amateur sailors, birdwatchers and scampering children the broad mouth of the Exe wears a smile.

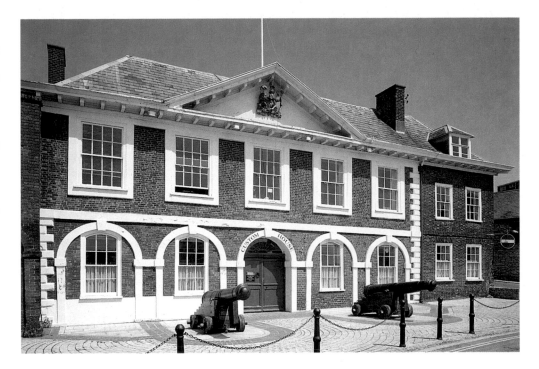

CUSTOMS HOUSE, EXETER, DEVON

The River Exe was tidal, and navigable up to Exeter, until 1282 when the Countess of Devon, keen to avenge some slight by the citizens of Exeter, built a weir right across the river below the town. Another three hundred years passed before Exeter could fully restore its waterfront traffic by driving its own ship canal to the open Exe estuary below Countess Weir. Prosperity flowed in, reflected in the graceful Customs House which was built on the quay in 1678–81. This trim, dignified house was the first brick building in Exeter, its bricks said to have been brought across from Holland as ships' ballast.

The West Country

A naval patrol vessel (training cadets from the town's famous Royal Naval College) scoots down the River Dart at Dartmouth across the track of the Kingswear-to-Dartmouth ferry. There's never a quiet moment on the Dart here, and hasn't been since the great musterings for the Crusades back in the twelfth century which brought Dartmouth into being. Newfoundland cod, Mediterranean trade and naval supply made the river-port town prosperous through the centuries, and filled its streets with superb buildings, many of which still stand.

Bayard's Cove, seen along the shore in the photograph, is where Dartmouth's visitors go for atmosphere: narrow, steep passageways, cobbled lanes, and a crooked waterfront with Tudor houses. Low on the shore stands Bearscove Castle (also known as Bayard's Castle), another fort built by King Henry VIII to counter the feared French invasion of the 1540s.

*O*f all five sections of coastline in this book, it is the West Country that most heavily relies on tourism. To very many holidaymakers the coastal villages, ports and harbours *are* the West Country, the very soul of Devon, Cornwall and Somerset. Coming to the cliff-encircled toe of England, people tend to gravitate, as if pressed outward by centrifugal force, to the coastline, rather than seeking out the rural pleasures inland. After all, what do visitors demand of a West Country holiday? A good supply of sunshine, a sparkling sea, a sandy beach with rockpools and great green Atlantic surfing rollers crashing in; and, above all, a snug little fishing village perched charmingly in a cleft of the cliffs, with fishing boats bobbing by a granite quay and a picturesque cluster of cottages spread along steep, cobbled streets and alleyways. The coastline of Devon and Cornwall is thick with such places: Mevagissey, Gorran Haven, Portloe, Pendower, Portscatho and St Mawes, for example, between St Austell and Truro; and St Ives, Portreath, Perranporth, Trenance, Trevan, Polzeath in one short stretch of the north coast of Cornwall. The old fishing and smuggling harbour of Polperro might have been created expressly for tourism, so well does it meet these romantic and eagerly held expectations.

Most inhabitants of Cornish coastal communities – the hardest pressed by tourism – will tell you firstly that they don't much care for the 'grockles', as they call the tourists, from June to September when they are as thick as flies round a jam pot and 'take us over'; and secondly that from June to September is when all the money is made that carries the village through the empty winter months. Youngsters find those winter months dead and boring, because to them the tourists are a breath of fresh air, while older folk enjoy getting their village and workplace back to themselves again. Obvious seeds of friction are here, between the different generations of Cornish people, and between them and the tourists. And then there are the incomers, who buy up the old salting cellars and turn them into craft shops, or set up artist's studios in sail lofts, or take over pubs and hotels. Cornish men and women have a long history of desperately hard work, as tin miners, granite quarriers, lead smelters, fishermen: work usually carried out in cold, wet, dark and dangerous conditions. The generations who underwent this kind of sweated labour are fast disappearing, but so much poverty and hardship in the past seems to have left a stamp of intransigence, independence and intolerance of outsiders across a large number of present-day Cornish characters. Devon and Somerset people, maybe thanks to their counties' kinder, more wooded and richly green interior landscape, appear less put out by their millions of visitors.

To the holidaymaker, part of the great charm of the West Country is that traditional work – especially fishing – and tourism go hand-in-hand in the fishing villages. Teignmouth boats don't go from Devon to Newfoundland after cod these days, nor do the fishermen of Newquay and Mevagissey haul in catches of hundreds of thousands of pilchards, as in the great eighteenth and nineteenth century days. But at Plymouth and Looe, Newlyn and Bideford there are thriving fishing fleets and fish markets, going about their daily business right outside the windows of the quayside trinket shops.

The West Country ports and docks, too, have had to change their style as traditional industries have sickened or died. Copper ore, granite and tin no longer fill the coasters at Porthleven and Penzance, but ball clay goes in quantities from Teignmouth, and china clay (admittedly, only a little) from tiny Charlestown; fertilizers come in to Bideford Quay, and Channel Island fruit to Torquay. Many of these hard-working industrial ports lie in lonely surroundings, up wooded rivers and winding creeks, spread up and along dramatic cliffs, backed by rolling fields and downland. In the West Country a working waterfront is part of the attraction for a visitor.

Silting is not quite so much of a problem for harbours and ports in this area of hard granites and deep-water quayside anchorages. Storm damage is a perennial hazard, though, when the south-west gales come roaring up the Channel from Biscay Bay and the Atlantic. South-west facing fishing harbours like Porthleven combat the weather with granite walls and defences of such enormous weight that it would take a Cornish giant to shift them.

These winter gales apart, the south-west peninsula has such a mild climate that Mediterranean flowers and shrubs grow happily at Penzance and in sheltered Torbay. With that gentle spring and summer weather, the beautiful location, the proximity of the coast to everywhere inland, the dashing history of Drake and Nelson, the thrilling

THE GANNEL, CORNWALL

This view looks seaward down the Gannel estuary, over the sand dunes of Crantock Beach. Here at the mouth of The Gannel, low water exposes vast stretches of sand. These sands choked off the life of the medieval port that once stood here. Legend says that they may once have put paid to far greater splendours. Either here, or under nearby Penhale Sands, lies the golden city of Langarrow, a Cornish Sodom, buried under a cataclysmic sandstorm as a punishment for the wickedness of its inhabitants. The medieval name for Crantock was 'Lancrantoc' – similar enough to Langarrow to point to the true site? Dig down deep into Crantock Beach – if you strike gold, the case is proven.

SALTASH, CORNWALL

'I. K. BRUNEL ENGINEER 1859' says the legend above the eastern portal of the Royal Albert Bridge, which towers over the village of Saltash and takes the railway across the River Tamar between Devon and Cornwall. At the time the bridge opened Brunel was far and away the most celebrated engineer in Britain, but he was also a man of contrasts: a Corinthian with an unequalled tally of engineering triumphs to his name (bridges, railways, tunnels, docks and steamships); a passionate man locked into a formal, nearly emotionless marriage; and a lover of cigars and good company who became a relentless workaholic and loner. The Royal Albert Bridge turned out to be his monument, for Brunel was dying even as it opened, worn out completely by his almost single-handed efforts to finish and launch his third and greatest steamship, *Great Eastern*. He was too weak to do more than lie and allow himself to be carried over the Tamar under the great tubular arcs. Within a few months Brunel was dead. How he would have loved to have been around to see this High Speed Train.

tales of shipwrecking and smuggling, it only needed the coming of the railways in early Victorian times to set the West Country's coastline on a profitable tourist track along which it still runs. Cheap 'fun in the sun' charter flights pose a threat, stealing away trade to the guaranteed sunshine and cheap booze of Spain and Greece. Those tourists who return later with their own young children to the security of the Cornish seaside they knew in childhood sometimes discover that they have been spoiled beyond tolerance of rainy days or unsophisticated entertainment. That's why the port authorities, the handlers of goods, the pilots and coastguards, the lighthouse keepers and fishermen, from Exeter down to Land's End and back up to Bristol, all have tourism and tourists' expectations as much in their minds as their own occupations. Business is second nature, even on the gorgeous West Country coastline where so many people come to escape and put all that behind them.

TEIGNMOUTH, DEVON

Teignmouth (pronounced 'Tinm'th') stands where the River Teign flows through its harbour basin into Babbacombe Bay. With wooded hills sheltering the harbour and a mild climate, Teignmouth is a popular sailing spot, but the river also handles large vessels which bring in wood pulp for paper making and take out ball clay. At low tide the basin of Teignmouth harbour is almost empty of water, exposing the large flat known as The Salty. Shifting sand banks and bars make this a place where helmsmen, skippers and pilots have to work closely together to manoeuvre the big ships safely through the narrow navigable channels.

TORQUAY, DEVON

A ferry of Torbay Seaways enters the harbour at Torquay after an evening crossing from the Channel Islands. Torquay, built like Rome on seven hills, has grown into a great seaside resort – a far cry from its days as a victualling and supply village for the British fleet during the Napoleonic Wars, when Torbay was the Channel's most important sheltered anchorage in rough weather. Many naval officers' wives brought their families to settle here in order to have as much time as possible with their men during shore leaves. Torquay's climate, often more Mediterranean than English, was good for sufferers from that very nineteenth-century disease, consumption; the benign weather and dramatic coastal scenery attracted first invalids and then those with good health and plenty of money. Torquay relaxed gently on to the bed of velvet on which it still reclines.

NOSS MAYO, DEVON

The view from Newton Ferrers to Noss Mayo across a creek of the River Yealm on an evening low tide is one of those little Devon treats. The village clusters round its church, built in 1882 by the squire, Lord Revelstoke, and the sheltered anchorage, tucked away among the woods a few miles south-east of Plymouth, is a favourite with yachtsmen in the know. The thick woods around the houses hold a number of splendid oaks as well as some fine specimens of ilex, the oak's evergreen cousin, whose shapely canopy rises from a trunk cracked into squares like crocodile skin.

PLYMOUTH, DEVON

Plymouth's long miles of waterfront look out to where Devon meets Cornwall. Here five rivers – Tamar, Tavy, Lynher, Plym and Yealm – all mingle in Plymouth Sound. Sutton Harbour, or Sutton Pool, shown here, is a narrow horseshoe-shaped basin at the centre of the old Plymouth of medieval streets, from which the poor storm-tossed Pilgrim Fathers finally managed to make a decisive getaway in *Mayflower* on 6 September 1620, leaving little *Speedwell* behind. Sutton Pool is one of the liveliest parts of a lively city, with a lot of activity gathered round the fishing boats and nearby fish market. Here stands the Customs House of 1810, its ground floor colonnade and arched upstairs windows giving it a look of permanent surprise – perhaps at its own good fortune in having survived the widespread destruction of the Second World War bombing raids on Plymouth.

LOOE, CORNWALL

The seven-arched granite bridge upriver from Looe's harbour, seen in the distance, was built in 1853 to replace a fifteenth-century bridge. That one had thirteen arches and a little hermitage chapel right in the middle, and connected the riverside settlements of West and East Looe. Looe is one of the most important fishing centres in the south of England. Shark fishing is a very popular pastime, as are inshore trips after mackerel and conger, but it's the commercial fleet that keeps the place humming. Several dozen trawlers operate out of Looe in the mackerel season, some of them owned and crewed by 'Scotsmen and them from up north', whose own North Sea grounds are so quickly being fished out. There's a daily auction of fresh fish in the fish market, built on the quay in 1987 in response to the boom – a cheering story amid so much general decline in Britain's fishing.

POLPERRO, CORNWALL

Beautiful Polperro is too beautiful for its own good in the summer season. You catch Polperro at its very best on a morning or evening in spring or autumn, when the jostling crowds have gone from its charming but extremely narrow streets. Polperro's situation is uncompromisingly picturesque, tumbling down a narrow gully in cliffs that rise to 400ft. The old smuggling village looks on to a harbour where a little inshore fishing keeps a precarious toe-hold among the 'gifte shoppes' and 'piskie grottoes'. The three-storey cottages reflect Polperro's fishing tradition in their specialised construction. The ground floors were built as cellars for salting and storing fish, and the fishermen's families reached their first-floor living quarters by outside flights of stone steps.

CHARLESTOWN, CORNWALL

The diminutive octagonal harbourmaster's office stands on the quayside at Charlestown, a port designed in the 1790s by the great harbour engineer John Smeaton for local landowner Sir Charles Rashleigh, and named after its originator. Planned as St Austell's outlet for tin, Charlestown harbour was soon taking wagonloads of china clay from the nearby diggings. Lorries still bring in the white powder or sludge to be tipped into the small boats that are all the tiny harbour can handle. But the large, sophisticated china clay docks at neighbouring Par have virtually robbed little Charlestown of its trade and its *raison d'être*.

MEVAGISSEY, CORNWALL

Stilt-like supports keep the fishing boats in Mevagissey harbour upright at their quayside moorings as the falling tide lowers the water level beneath their hulls. The harbour faces east, which ensures Mevagissey fishermen a launch when south- and west-facing harbours are closed for days by winter gales. Fishing still dominates Mevagissey, as it did in the great days of the pilchard fishery. Four thousand tons of the 'silver darlings' were exported in 1724 when the Catholic countries of Europe were gobbling up all the penitential pilchards they could get. As at Polperro, many of the fishermen's cottages were built tall to give ground-floor space for storing fish and fishing gear.

A few pilchards are still found inshore, but in insufficient numbers and at too low a price to be worthwhile. The smaller boats go after mackerel in winter, the larger ones after whitefish varieties all year round.

TRURO, CORNWALL

Drying at low water to a fast-running channel, the Truro River snakes its way from Cornwall's capital city between great sand flats to join the River Fal at the head of an estuary that pokes out creeks and side channels in all directions. Medieval Truro grew fat on the export of tin and iron ore, then on its fame as a fashionable eighteenth-century resort for the ailing rich – Cornwall's Bath. The towering cathedral, the first to be built in England since Sir Christopher Wren's St Paul's, was started in 1890. Its three spires were donated to the cathedral in memory of monarchs who had just died – the central 250ft Victoria Spire in 1901 and the Edward and Alexandra spires on the western towers in 1910, the year the cathedral itself was finished.

GWEEK, CORNWALL

The Helford River pushes westward into the Lizard peninsula from Falmouth Bay, throwing off muddy creeks to north and south as it goes. At the head of the river is the silted-up creek that once brought coal ships up to Gweek quay. It carried tin away, too – a trade that perhaps dates as far back as two thousand years; indeed, the name Gweek is said to derive from the Latin *vicus*, meaning a street, village or hamlet. Tin moulds several hundred years old are cut into some of the stone blocks built into the walls of the quay. The Cornish Seal Sanctuary was founded here in 1958, but little besides yacht halyards stirs these days at quiet, greenly rural Gweek.

PORTHLEVEN, CORNWALL

Sited on the north-west side of the Lizard peninsula and facing directly south-west into the teeth of Cornwall's worst weather, Porthleven's harbour only functions thanks to the protection of these massive granite walls and their lock gates, which together guard the inner harbour basin. They were constructed in the 1850s, after storms had destroyed a harbour built just after the Napoleonic Wars to allow Helston, three miles inland, an outlet for its copper ore and quarried stone. On Porthleven's solid granite quays stand old fish cellars and salting sheds. Not far away are their modern equivalents, the canning and deep-freezing plants that employ many local people. The fishermen themselves, though, still rely for their safety and regular employment on the confident craftsmanship of the Victorian masons who built these heroic harbour walls.

ST MICHAEL'S MOUNT, CORNWALL

St Michael's Mount stands in a wind-whipped sea, its causeway sunk beneath green Atlantic rollers, its back in the path of an approaching cloud-burst. The reward for climbing up the steep, cobbled street to the 230ft summit of the Mount is one of England's best coastal views, right around the thirty-mile arc of Mount's Bay. St Michael's Mount, protected by the tides and its superb early-warning outlook, has been a centre of commercial activity as well as a refuge since pre-Roman times when traders from Rome and Gaul knew it as Ictis, the isle where they could meet the local tribesmen and barter for their tin. The Benedictine monks of Mont St Michel in Normandy, an almost identical twin, built the monastery here when granted the site by Edward the Confessor. Church and castle came later, making the Mount into a hybrid – half fortification and half holy ground.

PENZANCE, CORNWALL

The Sail Training Association's flagship *Sir Winston Churchill* seeks shelter from a storm at Penzance's quayside. This 300-ton, three-masted topsail schooner has been taking crews of youngsters (and not-so-youngsters) all round the British coastline, across the North Sea and further afield ever since she left her Yorkshire makers in 1966. With all sail set she carries fourteen sails, and is usually crewed by thirty-nine eager, apprehensive trainees.

Penzance's east-facing harbour looks out into Mount's Bay below the freckling of handsome Georgian houses that tin prosperity built in the town, and the grand Victorian houses that resort prosperity brought in the wake of Isambard Kingdom Brunel's Great Western Railway in 1859. The year of the great engineer's death saw the birth of Penzance as the heart of the 'Cornish Riviera'.

NEWLYN, CORNWALL

Newlyn's fishing harbour looks across the little bay of Gwavas Lake to Penzance. For many years Cornwall's leading port for landing fish, Newlyn's fleet of mackerel trawlers goes out to deep-sea grounds during the winter season. The fortunes of the port have been in gentle decline for decades. In 1937 the picturesque old fishermen's quarter, which had drawn such eminent painters to the village that there was a recognized school of Newlyn artists, was demolished by order of 'planners' on Penzance Council with more reforming zeal than long-sighted commonsense; this in spite of a spirited protest by the Newlyn fishermen, who sailed a lugger round to Westminster to make their point. However, there are still enough cobbled alleys and working fishing boats and gear in Newlyn to please any artist. The village has another claim to fame: all Ordnance Survey heights in Britain are calculated from its sea level.

LAND'S END, CORNWALL

Looking appropriately like a castle's fortified walls, the sea-bitten granite stacks of Land's End guard the south-western toe of Cornwall. From here on a clear day you can see the Scilly Isles, twenty-eight miles away. Somewhere off Land's End lies the fabled land of Lyonesse, overwhelmed according to legend by a gigantic wave. In stormy weather, so local people say, you can hear the golden bells of Lyonesse tolling beneath the waves. Land's End, although nowadays privately owned and geared for tourism, still breathes mystery and romance for its visitors – the very tip of Britain.

ST IVES, CORNWALL

This early morning shot of St Ives – so early that the sands are deserted – illustrates well the appeal of the town to artists who have adored it since Turner came to paint in 1811. Their names read like a rollcall of artistic honour – Whistler, Sickert, Munnings, Bernard Leach, Ben Nicolson, Barbara Hepworth, to name only a handful. Today the magic lingers: on a sunny morning you can hardly move around the harbour without knocking into an easel. But things have got more sophisticated, and rowdier. The town's narrow streets carry too many cars, and the little branch railway does what branch railways did all over the country before Dr Beeching took his axe to them – it brings holidaymakers to the seaside here. Meanwhile a little fishing goes on from the pier, built, like Charlestown's (but nearly thirty years earlier), by John Smeaton.

NEWQUAY, CORNWALL

The projecting headland of Towan Head, from which this view was taken, provides effective shelter for Newquay's harbour from the west. Newquay was known to be a good place for a fishing fleet to base itself as long ago as 1440, when a harbour wall was built here. The present harbour was built in 1838, and when a goods railway opened in 1874 it became a very busy place, handling the export of china clay. But the event for which destiny had been grooming Newquay took another two years to arrive: the coming of the passenger railway. Subsequently the town mushroomed into the archetypal Victorian Cornish resort of cream teas, clean sands and big surfing waves.

THE HUER'S HOUSE, NEWQUAY, CORNWALL

More like something out of Nazareth than Newquay, this strange, rugged building stands out on Towan Head high above Newquay's bay, its past an enigma to local historians. Some say it dates no further back than the early nineteenth century, others that it was built as long ago as 1300. It may originally have been a hermit's cell, or a store-house, or a primitive kind of lighthouse. What is certain is that when Newquay and the other Cornish fishing villages were cashing in on the great shoals of pilchards of the eighteenth and nineteenth centuries, men known as 'huers' (from the old Cornish word *hevva*, meaning a school of fish) would stand up here on the roof of the house every autumn, watching for the incoming pilchard shoals. When they were spotted, the huer would bellow, '*Hevva! Hevva!*', wave his arms or a flag, blow a trumpet and do all he could to alert the fishermen on the beach below.

PADSTOW, CORNWALL

Once past Padstow's Doom Bar, you couldn't wish for a more sheltered anchorage, or a more pleasant, old-fashioned town in which to idle away a day. If that day happens to be May Day, a different side of Padstow will be on show. On that day the two Padstow 'Obby 'Osses, the Red Ribbon and the Blue Ribbon, are let loose on the town. Padstow May Day is a celebration which pulls everyone in the town together, as the flower-decked crowds follow the devilish 'Osses and their partners, the High-Stepping Teasers, all singing:

> Unite and unite, and let us all
>   unite,
> For summer is a-come unto
>   day;
> And whither we are going we
>   will all unite
> In the merry morning of May!

MORWENSTOW, CORNWALL

The Vicarage Cliffs at Morwenstow are the last magnificent exclamation of the north Cornwall coastline before it hands over to Devon. Magnificent, too, were the generosities, eccentricities and failings of the Rev. Robert Stephen Hawker, who reigned as Vicar of Morwenstow for forty years, from 1834 to 1875. At the age of nineteen he married his forty-one-year-old godmother. He went on his parish visits with a trained pig in tow. He quarrelled with the church authorities. He pinched babies at the font to make them yell the Devil out. He wore fishermen's thigh-boots, a fisherman's jersey marked with a cross where the spear wounded Christ, a brimless hat, a long red coat and a billowing yellow cloak. He remarried, at sixty, a Polish girl of twenty, and had three children by her. And . . . he was a kind, humane man, a poet who wrote on these cliffs and a generous friend.

BIDEFORD, DEVON

The ancient trading port of Bideford sits attractively above the wide estuary of the River Torridge, spanned by the twenty-four arches of the fifteenth-century Bideford Bridge, 600ft long. Seafaring atmosphere clings seductively to the quiet streets, steep and narrow alleyways and dark old quayside pubs of the little town, from which local men set off to crew the ships of the great Elizabethan explorers – Drake, Hawkins, Raleigh and Grenville. Charles Kingsley stayed in the Royal Hotel at the eastern end of Bideford Bridge while he was writing *Westward Ho!* in the 1850s.

ILFRACOMBE, DEVON

In wonderfully dramatic and lovely natural surroundings Ilfracombe was a sure-fire success as a genteel resort when the fashion caught on along the north Devon coastline at the beginning of the nineteenth century. Starved of Continental travel by that wretched little Bonaparte, the gentlefolk came flocking to the 'Awesome Splendours' of north Devon in response to the siren calls of Romantics like William Wordsworth and Samuel Taylor Coleridge. Paddle steamers from Bristol and the South Wales ports had diluted the Ilfracombe gentry with coarser persons long before the railway came up from Barnstaple in 1874. Squeezed and bundled up together in their constricted site, the Ilfracombe houses and hotels built in those great Victorian golden days seem even larger and more magnificent, like jewels in a green and blue setting.

LANTERN HILL, ILFRACOMBE, DEVON

On the hundred-foot summit of Lantern Hill in centre stage of Ilfracombe harbour, the fourteenth-century Chapel of St Nicholas still shows a red light at night to guide in fishermen and warn off passing boats – a light maintained in the chapel by Ilfracombe's Rotarians, who restored the building in 1962. The chapel, a lighthouse since the early sixteenth century, has suffered some strange incarnations. At various times, in addition to its religious and custodial duties, it has seen service as a laundry, a practice hall for the town band, and a home for a couple and their fourteen children.

WATERMOUTH, DEVON

The glorious coastline of Exmoor presents a heart-lifting view, with those characteristic rounded, green clifftops descending to wrinkled coves full of caves and slanted strata of sandstone. Watermouth, a deep-water inlet running parallel with the cliffs inside the outlying projection of Widmouth Head, was probably burrowed out, like the nearby Valley of Rocks, by a river blocked with ice at the end of the last Ice Age. It forms a sheltered harbour for pleasure craft and the small inshore boats of local lobster fishermen.

LYNMOUTH, DEVON

Lynmouth lies cradled between the steep hills of Exmoor and the sea, everyone's dream picture of a lovely old seaside village. The East and West Lyn rivers gurgle peacefully together through the boulders of Lynmouth's beach. On 15 August 1952, however, they rose in fury on a pitch-black night and smashed a path of destruction through the village. Thirty-four people died in the disaster. The pretty little village street that you wander along today is a modern rebuilding. The red-topped Rhenish tower in the foreground, built to store sea water for a Victorian general's bath tub, was flattened in the flood, and subsequently reconstructed stone by stone. New flood defences ensure the future safety of one of north Devon's best-loved beauty spots.

MINEHEAD, SOMERSET

Minehead is a lively place in summer. The big holiday camp on the shore is partly responsible, but people were flocking to Minehead in Victorian times, too. The enormously wide, firm sands of the beach, giving off that proper seaweedy, salty smell, were always the main attraction. North Hill, the bulbous outlier of Exmoor that shelters Minehead Harbour from easterlies, made possible the town's earlier development as an importer of Irish wool for the Taunton weavers. The old medieval streets along the flank of the hill are still there above the Victorian resort buildings. With assets like these, allied to superb woodland running west to the nearby hills of Exmoor, the Quantock Hills to the east and the Brendons to the south, Minehead's popularity with West Country and Midland holidaymakers is easy to understand.

CLIFTON SUSPENSION BRIDGE, BRISTOL

The stately terraces of Clifton are joined to Leigh Woods by the Clifton Suspension Bridge above the Bristol Avon. Conceived by – who else? – Isambard Kingdom Brunel, begun by him in 1831, halted when the money ran out after the abutments were finished, and completed in 1864 (thirty-four years after work started, and five years after Brunel's death), the Clifton Suspension Bridge is one of several memorials in Bristol to the engineer whose Great Western Railway gave the city its nineteenth-century impetus. The statistics of the bridge are worth repeating, for they demonstrate the genius of Brunel, his grasp of the art of the possible: 245ft above high water level, 1352ft long and 702ft between the piers, 31ft wide, and made with 1500 tons of steel and chains salvaged from the old Hungerford Bridge in London. No-one else at that time could even have dreamed of tackling such a project.

SS *GREAT BRITAIN*, BRISTOL

Our final port of call on the journey round England's coastline is a fitting one. Isambard Kingdom Brunel's genius was never better displayed than in his revolutionary steamships. The 3618-ton *Great Britain*, when launched by Prince Albert at Bristol in 1843, was the world's first ocean-going iron ship to rely on screw propulsion. Twenty-one years later, after a varied career, she wound up on the beach at Sparrow Cove in the Falkland Islands, and lay there rotting. In 1970 she was floated halfway round the world, back to Wapping Dock in Bristol – the very dock from which she had been launched. She symbolises all the high purpose, the inventiveness, the practicality – the sheer refusal to be beaten – of her creator, elements that characterize not only the energy and optimism so typical of Bristol but also the working life and history of England's coastline.

Photographer's Notes

It was at Wells in north Norfolk that I first contemplated a book on the subject of the ports and harbours around the coast of England. Here at spring tides 700-ton coasting freighters inch their way up the shallow channel between marshes and wheat-fields to tie up, sometimes two deep, along the little stone quay. The wheat-sheaves and fishes which occupy opposing quarters of the town's coat-of-arms perfectly symbolize that intermingling of land and sea which was to become the dominant theme of my work on this project. Later, on the estuary of the River Dart below Totnes, bleating sheep and the harsh cries of the herring-gull were to tell the same story in a different medium.

At Wells the cargo is grain and animal feeds, at Deptford scrap-metal, and at Newhaven sand and gravel – pretty mundane stuff. But for all their diesel motors and electronic communications systems, I see these little freighters as the linear descendents of all those humble vessels which for hundreds of years have carried goods not more glamorous then these over the oceans of the world. And I cannot forget that even in fair conditions the coastline of the British Isles, with its sandbanks, its rocks and sluicing tides, demands respect. In foul weather these are hostile shores indeed: on one ghastly night in 1692 no fewer than 200 ships were lost in the bitter north-easterly gales which lashed the coast of north Norfolk; and in the disastrous storm which roared up the Channel on the night of 26–27 November 1703 some 8000 people, mostly seafarers, lost their lives, twelve warships being wrecked on the Goodwin Sands alone. But the courage, skill and persistence learned over centuries of fishing in the far west, or in negotiating the sandbanks of the Thames estuary, took English mariners to all the corners of the globe. And for each of the great men whose achievements are recounted in the history books there were thousands who toiled at sea unknown. Their names, like Keats's, are writ in water.

The collection of material for this book has continued intermittently for some five years. The film used was Ektachrome Professional roll-film in its 220 guise, which gives sixteen 2¼ × 3¼ in. (6 × 9 cm) exposures per film. Filters were used only to correct the colour cast inherent in the film batches concerned, latterly at levels rather higher than I would have wished. The camera generally used was a Fujica 690 with 100 mm and 150 mm lenses. Architectural views were taken with a Gandolfi camera made to my specification in 1969 for the rather reasonable sum of £35; this is similar to a cigar-box (but ebonised black, of course), with a rising front panel carrying a 65 mm Super-Angulon lens in a focusing mount. I find the use of the appropriate equipment to banish those dreadful converging verticals so much more practical than the expedients sometimes employed.

Oh, and my favourite among the ports and harbours of old England? Penzance.

Index

Page numbers in *italics* refer to illustrations.